Cold Email Manifesto

ENDORSEMENTS

"Alex is the real deal, I've watched him write emails and get responses from Fortune 500 CEOs same day."

—Dennis Yu
Blitzmetrics

"Alex, just wanted to say thank you! Last month we had our best sales month ever. We did 10.5k in sales and this month I'm at 16k already and will probably hit around 20–25k this month."

—Matthew Fabrico
Agency Owner

"Alex, just want to thank you for the success you've already brought to my speaking business after learning your secrets about email outreach and marketing. From just our first hour [implementing your concepts] I've already generated 50k in business... ONE HOUR!! You're definitely a game-changer!"

—Magie Cook
CEO Magie's Salsa
(Acquired by Campbells)

COLD EMAIL
MANIFESTO

How to contact anyone, make more sales,
and take your company to the next level

ALEX BERMAN
ROBERT INDRIES

NEW YORK

LONDON • NASHVILLE • MELBOURNE • VANCOUVER

COLD EMAIL MANIFESTO

How to Contact Anyone, Make More Sales, and Take
Your Company to the Next Level

Published in New York, New York, by Morgan James Publishing. Morgan James is a
trademark of Morgan James, LLC. www.MorganJamesPublishing.com

Proudly distributed by Publishers Group West®

Morgan James BOGO™

A **FREE** ebook edition is available for you
or a friend with the purchase of this print book.

CLEARLY SIGN YOUR NAME ABOVE

Instructions to claim your free ebook edition:
1. Visit MorganJamesBOGO.com
2. Sign your name CLEARLY in the space above
3. Complete the form and submit a photo
   of this entire page
4. You or your friend can download the ebook
   to your preferred device

ISBN 9781636981376 paperback
ISBN 9781636981383 ebook
Library of Congress Control Number:
2023932380

Cover Design by:
Alex Berman

Interior Design by:
Chris Treccani
www.3dogcreative.net

Morgan James is a proud partner of Habitat for Humanity Peninsula
and Greater Williamsburg. Partners in building since 2006.

Get involved today! Visit: www.morgan-james-publishing.com/giving-back

TABLE OF CONTENTS

CHAPTER 1.

Starting From Scratch

Three dollars. I flew to Japan with just airline miles and three dollars in my pocket. How did it get to this point?

I had a startup at the time, which was worth $100 million. Well, I thought it was worth $100 million! I owned 10% of a lead generation cold email startup. I had a $10 million net worth and a $10 million lifestyle. My "cofounder" was paying me over $100K per year, we were living the absolute stereotype of Silicon Valley life. I was staying in the fanciest hotels, we were partying all of the time, it seemed like everything was going great.

Which brings us to Tokyo. One day, my business partner invited me to Japan to meet with some investors. He said, "This is the key to breaking into the Asian market!" This seemed fine at first. I paid for my own flight and got on the plane. Everything appeared perfectly normal, but then when I arrived he simply wasn't there. For two days I was wandering around Tokyo, waiting for this guy to show up, wondering what the what on earth I should do next.

Suddenly, out of the blue, he pinged me. "Where have you been?!" He was bizarrely pretending that I was the one avoiding him, which didn't make any sense! So I began to grill him on precisely what was going on with the Japanese investors, needless to say, they never materialized. It turned out to be complete BS.

By this time, I was completely sick of the situation, so I flew back home to my parents' house, using the last of my air miles gained from credit card hacking a few years before. When I said we were living the party lifestyle, I wasn't exaggerating. I wish I could say I was flat broke, but it was worse, I was over $40,000 in debt. Completely out of money. This might all sound a little worrying, but the worst, by a considerable distance, was yet to come.

This supposedly $100 million startup business, in which I had invested everything over the last six months of my life, was built on a house of cards. And this guy I knew as William the CEO was a pretty busy gentleman. I soon discovered that he was also Kevin, the Chief of Operations. And Jeff the lead content creator. And four more employees. The company was a total phantom.

And on top of all that, while I was selling all these supposed deals for this potentially massive company — I closed over $1 million in under 6 months — the apparent CEO of the company wasn't delivering any of the work.

So the rock bottom point of my life was when I was at my parents' house, completely broke, with absolutely no money. The wool had been pulled over my eyes, and now clients were calling me concerning this defunct company because the CEO had vanished completely. He just stopped responding to emails. Not surprisingly, everyone wanted their money back... and I was the face of the brand. Money that I didn't have because William owned the bank accounts.

But sometimes the greatest gifts that you receive in life come carefully disguised as your worst nightmares. I am thankful for going through that experience, as it made me realize that I needed to get my life on track. I quit drinking immediately. Chucked the partying in the garbage and vowed to turn things around.

The good news is that I built up a significant amount of important and valuable experience. I'd sold millions of dollars in mobile app and website development and millions in lead generation services. I'd worked with some major brands; for example, at one point I was working on social media for a major chicken company. But I burned the candle at both ends, and I realized that I had absolutely nothing to show for my achievements. I was over

$40,000 in debt, after having the delusional belief that I was worth $10 million! So that was a kick in the teeth and a wake-up call in anyone's language! Paper net worth is not net worth.

After a little reflection on the situation, I called my friend Robert who had been working on a content marketing agency. And after throwing around a few ideas, we realized that we needed to go big. This was the turning point of my life.

From that moment, we began sending out cold emails, these are messages written to people you don't know offering them your service. We started with digital agencies, pitching them on marketing services. I built a list of leads and from the first 20 cold emails I sent, we made $10,000.

From there it just kept growing and we closed over $600,000 in 2 months. And I realized that cold email is the ultimate safety net. Whatever happens in your life, however low you fall, no matter what problems you encounter, you can dig your way out of it with cold email.

I'm now fully confident that I can use a free email account and some well-written text to get out of any monetary problem. I retired the second we got that first response. I realized that if I could master cold email, I'd never have money problems again.

This works in every walk of life, all over the world, regardless of any demographics.

But you have to get it right.

PAINFUL MISTAKES

Needless to say, not everyone is getting it right! My company and I have now worked with hundreds of business owners. Most of these have been service agencies and Software as service startups. And one of the biggest mistakes that we see made repeatedly is that the distribution model is completely messed up before the company is launched.

Generally, people believe that they need to get big-name influencers talking about them or spend hundreds of thousands of dollars on ads, and because of that will pay an absolute fortune for this privilege. That's a massive mistake. The second big mistake that we encounter is owners of service-based businesses completely rely on referrals to grow the business.

You'd be surprised how some successful businesses handle their marketing. For example, I collaborated with an agency in Boston a few years ago, a company that generated $20 million annually in revenue, and worked with a ton of major brands. I was assessing their operation, so I asked them how they attract clients. And they told me that it was entirely based on referrals. They literally had no client acquisition process! The entire sales team was inbound, meaning that nobody was actually pushing the business, and they still made $20 million off-the-table scraps that got thrown their way!

And yes, I must confess, somehow that worked for them! They obviously said grace to the right people! But their approach is a complete lottery. It might have worked for them so far, but their potential to grow the business is essentially zero. If you're just relying on referrals as an agency owner, it's akin to moving to Hollywood to become an actor. Yes, it's not completely inconceivable that you might end up on the silver screen, but the odds are more than one in a million.

So what's the solution to this poorly founded approach? Quite simple. You need to be growing via outbound marketing. And that's why cold email is an excellent way to grow your business, and I would argue the ideal solution for any business that sells to other businesses (B2B).

First, if you rely on referrals, an outbound email will attract way more referrals. Let's say, for example, you're working with Sony; the people at Sony may recommend you to other entertainment companies. But if you wanted to change your niche completely, perhaps you might want to move into e-commerce, then it's much easier to reach out to these people and tell them that you've worked with Sony, rather than waiting for Sony to do this for you. Unfortunately, you might find that people at Sony have better things to do!

So if you're not pushing this angle, you're wasting a huge amount of potential. Every deal and every customer that you attract through outbound could deliver three or four more referrals. Even a highly successful agency, like the aforementioned $20 million revenue company, can add clients in a very short timeframe. They could become a $60 million agency in under 6 months, just by sending a few dozen emails a week. And those results are not unrealistic.

We just talked about agencies, now let's dive into SaaS — software as a service. If you're in sales for a software business, you are competing in a saturated advertising space. That is baked into the cake. You are vying for space with every other funded startup all over the world, along with many major established companies. We're talking billions of dollars per year being spent to get customers to buy from them instead of you. So if you want to stand out from the crowd, you're either going to have to pay a ton of money to compete head-to-head, or else no one is ever going to see you. Either that or you're back to those million-to-one odds again.

Instead, I would advise sending targeted cold emails, booking sales meetings, and winning based on personalization.

While the big guys spam, you win by hitting potential customers with highly targeted, customized cold emails.

MISCONCEPTIONS AND REALITY

So the big question that you might have at this point is why massive and successful companies ignore, or at least neglect, cold email? And I think a lot of it is purely down to perception.

People believe that cold email is spam. They have all sorts of mental blocks. Perhaps some people believe that it will be a nuisance. For example, I was speaking with an artist recently, who has approximately 40,000 followers on Instagram. So I told him that he should reach out to Nike, and other big companies that are likely to work with a creative person. And, of course, he concluded that I was completely correct — in fact, he was so thankful for the idea, that he offered to buy me a nice dinner. And, of course, when I checked in two weeks later he never did anything about it! Not a single email was sent or dinner was purchased. Gary, I'm still waiting for that prime rib...

If you follow the information in this book, I can provide you with the perfect scripts, I can tell you exactly what niche you should be targeting, I can tell you exactly how to go about it, and most importantly — I can assure you that you will grow your business and your revenue. That is 100% guaranteed if you're willing to invest a little effort in the process.

If you put these big companies on a pedestal and make them sacred cows, you'll never get anywhere. You have to realize that they're ultimately comprised of people. They still bleed red blood and have to go to bed at night! Just because they're big, just because they're successful does not mean that they're immune to good marketing or valuable products and services. Quite the opposite.

What is really cool about the system that I will outline in this book is that it doesn't involve spamming. It's about sending 15–20 emails at any given time, which are highly personalized towards people that require the service or software that you're providing. This direct targeting simply works and will continue to work for the next 50 years, regardless of any changes in technology, spam detection, algorithms, or anything else.

The fascinating thing about cold email is that one person pitching to another is the way that business has always been done. It's how deals are done — from billionaires meeting potential investors to film studios putting together the latest action thriller. Every deal starts with a well-craft mail. And that's all we're doing here. What we're doing is perfectly natural and proven, which is why it has achieved and will continue to achieve excellent results.

NEVER TOO LATE TO CHANGE

That brings me to another important point about this email system. It's never too late to change, and it's certainly never too late to implement cold email marketing. This system will work today, it will work tomorrow, and it will work for the rest of your life. So getting on board is something that will deliver a short-term increase in sales, and it's something that you can then use repeatedly for as long as you wish.

I believe that most successful people have a profound transformative experience. And it's usually a low rather than a high. We all have to go through that experience in order to be set on the right path. In order to believe that we've been as low as it's possible to go. It's at this point that we experience true freedom, because, as a famous old song goes, "freedom is just another word for nothing left to lose."

I had another of those transformative experiences quite recently. At the time, my co-founder and I realized that we needed to own equity in successful companies. So we started doing what we know; cold emailing the guys that we admire. Of course, they all responded, because we're cold email experts!

So we got down to talking with them and asked for pieces of their companies. I was on a call with a mentor, let's change his name to Allan, who was and is a real inspiration for me. I was in a Las Vegas hotel room, chatting away, and he seemed to be enthused by the prospect of giving me a piece of his company. It all looked so promising. By the end of the call, and I was there with my little brother at the time, we were all so hyped about joining the company. My brother was like: "Dude, does that happen all the time? Did he really just give you a $20 million company for free?!"

Anyway, fast forward two weeks... and we didn't get any piece of the company! We were completely ghosted. But we thought: "Okay, we're not going to give up!". So we tried again.

I sent some more cold emails, and we got more bites. We met with another major SaaS company, one that was particularly successful. The board of this company had absolutely no idea who we were, and they didn't respond favorably when we asked for equity. So then we started cold emailing again, to people who were ranked highly on Product Hunt, top founders, in an attempt to buy equity. And we got absolutely nowhere. That was the last time that I felt like a failure and the point where I realized that I needed to improve further still. I had come a significant distance, but the journey definitely wasn't over.

But just like any sales campaign, if you keep sending and improving you will win. And we did eventually convince someone to give us half of their company, an awesome guy who has a 7-figure outreach agency and a 7-figure SaaS startup. A partner who completely believes in us. And we didn't have to pay him anything. He gave us 50% equity purely in exchange for us working with him to help grow the company. All we did was ensure that we stood out from the crod, and that we are someone he simply must work with. So even when things don't work out, it doesn't matter. It's all just a learning experience. Where there's life there's hope, and you can just pick yourself up, dust yourself off, and start again.

But none of that learning would have happened without cold email — this one skill was the reason we were able to land enough meetings to get to that successful acquisition. Without it, we might have given up when Allan turned us down. Instead, we were able to use cold email to acquire a company with no money down! That's the power and flexibility that comes with getting good at cold email.

It's amazing…nothing is stopping you, except one thing…

MASTERING MINDSET

Your mindset and mentality are key. It's critical to success in cold emailing. They are critical to success in any field.

It's extremely important to remain positive, and to ensure that any setbacks don't alter your determination or outlook. You are going to get more rejections in this field than leads. I can promise you that! And that applies to any field. You have to be ready to view this process as an experience, as a journey, as a stepping stone to your ultimate success. Anyone who has achieved any form of success in any field has either consciously or subconsciously absorbed this life lesson.

I was living in Florida. I had lost $10 million. I had to do my mom's laundry! That could have been the end. But not for one second did I think I was done. I didn't allow myself to sleep on the beach, or start a life of crime and drug dealing! I dusted myself off, turned myself around, and immediately started pushing forward again.

If you can internalize this lesson, really understand its value, and then incorporate it into your own life, I will make you a guarantee right now. You will win with cold emailing if you implement the system in this book. That's not 99% certain, it's 100% going to happen.

And the great thing about cold email is that there is absolutely no barrier to entry. There is no age barrier to entry, there is no race barrier to entry, there is no gender or location barrier to entry. I repeat, there is nothing stopping you! Behind the computer screen nobody knows what you look like — I've seen clients in India close $10,000 a month deals with American companies, I've seen minimum wage employees make hundreds of thousands of dollars within a few months. And it all starts with mastering the skill of cold email.

FLEXIBLE FOREVER

Another fantastic thing about cold email is that you can use it for the rest of your life. It can be used flexibly in so many different areas of your business, and even different areas of your life, always with the aim of improving and achieving goals. And it will never lose relevance, it will become something that you can continually implement for as long as you choose. You can start this right now, today, with absolutely zero barrier to entry, and you can continue cold emailing for the rest of your life, as long as you are still drawing breath!

You also don't need a network or any contacts to begin. Now that's an absolutely massive advantage. Historically, this barrier applied to every sector of business. You needed contacts to begin, or you needed to attract an audience and customer base extremely quickly. This was what fundamentally determined whether or not your business was successful.

To give you an example, McDonald's started with a single restaurant in San Bernardino, California. All they had was a good idea and a good product. They had to rely on word of mouth, and perhaps some minor and rather unsophisticated advertising. They had no way of contacting a large number of customers, they had no way of connecting with people who might fund them and help them grow, they couldn't even reasonably expect to contact successful people in other industries.

You can do all of that today. In fact, you would be stupid not to do it!

I first got into cold email because I was in college, with no immediate prospects. I had no contacts. I knew nobody. I was living in Naples, Florida, and studying for a marketing degree. And I don't mind admitting that I was a completely mediocre student. I was never going to become an esteemed academic! What I really wanted was a job in New York. But, again, I didn't know anyone in New York, and I had cut myself off financially from my parents after reading the book Millionaire Next Door. However, I didn't want these factors to prevent me from following my heart and my dreams.

So I made a list of companies that I wanted to work with, and then moved to New York City with no plan whatsoever. I had maybe $3,000 that I had saved up, so a small buffer against homelessness and destitution, but I'm sure you're aware that $3,000 doesn't get you very far in New York City!

There is something about the hive of activity that is Manhattan which makes you believe that you can succeed. There are so many people milling around in this enclosed space, you figure that it must be possible to sell something to some of them!

Every single day that I was in New York City, I would go to a coffee shop. And I would send 100 cold emails asking people to meet me for coffee. And within just three days of moving to New York, I met with Joe Zimmer, who was the marketing director at Betterment, which is now a hugely successful investment company, but they were just starting out back then. I also met with some people from WeWork, back before all the scandals.

Anyway, Joe introduced me to some more people, and I quickly began to build up a network of contacts. It was a perfect illustration of the fact that you can use cold email to smash through even what seem to be impossible barriers. People would have said that I was insane to do what I did, but I ended up getting a job within two weeks. I worked for a SaaS founded by a former investment banker, and later used the skills that I acquired there to get my first few clients.

This was the start of a journey that has already been pretty exciting, but which I genuinely believe is just beginning. I have used the processes and life lessons that I learned at that time to acquire businesses and generate revenue. I've used cold email to book speaking gigs. My cofounder Robert and I used it to grow our lead generation company X27 to 7 figures in revenue, and I've helped many other entrepreneurs as well.

One of our consulting clients, Maggie Cook, sold her company to Campbell's, the soup manufacturers, for $150 million. And Maggie was an orphan in Mexico, so she's well acquainted with poverty. She was a highly successful entrepreneur, but Maggie wasn't sure how to market herself as a speaker, so I helped her with her cold email strategy. We began with just 15 personalized emails to conference organizers. And within a couple weeks, literally weeks, she managed to book $80,000 worth of speaking gigs; it kick-started her entire speaking career, and completely changed her outlook on what's possible.

So it's important to emphasize that you can use this cold emailing system for anything. I have used it to grow my SaaS businesses, I've used it to get booked on hundreds of podcast interviews — for example, I've been on Entrepreneur on Fire twice; I think I'm one of around 10 people who have appeared more than once. Through cold emailing I've been featured in Entrepreneur, Huffington Post, and Forbes; in fact, I became a Forbes contributor through cold email. If you have something that you want to achieve in life, you can do it through the cold email system that we present in this book.

DEALING WITH PERCEPTION

One of the things you will inevitably run into with cold email is the suggestion that you're spamming. That just goes with the territory, especially when you're just starting out. And, trust me, you're going to hear much worse than that as well. For example, when I began cold emailing, I was told that one particular email that I sent was the worst that the recipient had ever read. But they still booked a call. They lectured me all about the quality of the email on the call. And then they bought.

The only thing that you can trust is that it's going to work out in the end, if you keep persisting, keep learning from your mistakes — checking your open rates, response rates, measuring — like a scientist, and believe in what you're doing. If you're ready to develop this unflinching self-belief, and actively receive feedback from the market, you will inevitably succeed.

The wrong way to react to someone telling you that you're spamming, is to send out 10,000 emails, and spam even harder! And yet, a lot of people do that.

Instead, a smarter approach would be to question why the recipient believes you're spamming. Is it because your email isn't personalized enough? Was it because the recipient is the wrong contact, and would never buy your product or service in a million years? If you ask yourself these key questions, you can then use this feedback to get better, so that you are no longer emailing people in a way that appears to be spam.

Eventually, you'll start to be praised for the quality of your emails, instead of being scolded. This initial phase of criticism is just another stepping stone from where you are right now on the path to where you need to reach. But you have to accept that this is part of the journey. Lots of people are going to hate you whatever you do, but you have to ignore this and remain fully convinced that your approach will work out.

REACHING $100 MILLION IN LEADS GENERATED

$100 million in leads is an impressive sales figure. It's a powerful milestone. But it's also an achievable goal. Especially with cold email. We have generated this figure for our clients at x27, and we would not have been able to do this if it was only based on luck. Cold Email is just a numbers game. So here is the multi-million dollar sales process.

First, when you're selling via e-mail you need to ensure that your product or service is priced correctly. As a general rule, I don't believe that cold email is the best way to go if your software project, product, or service is under $2,000, otherwise the time spent won't be worth it. But you can use this to sell anything from $2,000 up to millions or even billions of dollars.

This is a big mistake that a lot of people make, particularly in the SaaS space. They come in at $9 per month, and believe that cold email will work for their product, but at this price point you'd be better off running ads. But if you're selling a service like coding, design, marketing or a consulting package worth at least $2,000, that is where cold email can change your business.

Second, you need to ensure that you're selling something that is in extremely high demand. This means that you need to test your cold emails before you scale the process. And target effectively. What a lot of agency clients do is sell web and iOS development, along with other similar services, and they're willing to sell it to anyone. We've all seen these companies — want a website? They'll build it. How about a complex API? Sure. Designs for your business cards? They're great at it!

A business can succeed like that, but to really thrive, for each cold email, you need a specific offer and a specific customer.

The successful version of this is to phrase your offer in a hyper-specific way. Instead of saying "we build websites" say "we do Kubernetes consulting for startups that have over 2 million active users per month."

If you can lock in your offer and get hyper-specific, you can find millions of dollars in deals and you will massively outperform any business that attempts to do everything for everybody. You cannot be all things to all people. You must target clients the right way and hone in on the specific niche for your business and you will hugely magnify your success.

On a personal level, X27 made millions selling lead generation services to other agency owners. We discovered service business owners all need more business, so we honed in on that and became world class at finding new customers for them.

That's all it took. We identified a specific customer (agency owners), created a specific offer (lead generation via cold email), and pitched it to them using cold email. Then we repeated it over and over again.

So that's the process. Make sure you charge enough. Find out the exact offer that will appeal to your specific niche. The no-brainer offer that people will snap up immediately. Target effectively. Write a customized email script that will convert (we will discuss this as the book unfolds). And send 20 emails, using any number of cold email sending tools; there are dozens available, and you can get an up to date list by visiting ColdEmailManifesto.com/tools.

Then measure your results. If your open rate is disappointing, send another 20 with a different subject line. If you're happy with your open rate, but received no responses, keep your subject line, rewrite the body, and iterate over and over and over again, until you hit your benchmark stats. If you do this effectively, you should be able to achieve 4–8 meetings on your calendar for every hundred emails, and at the same time ramp up the number of emails you send. This will allow you to book unlimited qualified meetings for your business. And if you're an effective salesperson, then somewhere between one-third and half of these should turn into revenue — some people early on even have a 100% close rate.

If you're doing this effectively, selling a $10,000 service, and you really get it working, you'll be able to make two or more sales for every hundred emails. That's $20,000 in new business generated, just by sending a few emails!

STARTING WITH NOTHING

Many of you reading this book may be starting with nothing. No money, no clients, no experience. But that is absolutely no problem. I started in that position too.

There is a myth in Silicon Valley, and the entrepreneurship space in general, that software needs to be really expensive and fully developed. You need ads and sophisticated infrastructure to grow your business. But that's just not true.

You can use your lack of money as an advantage. I have seen dozens of entrepreneurs build a $3,000 software tool by hiring freelancers in third world countries. And then use cold email pitches to build the company up to $3,000 in monthly revenue. That can be achieved in a short timeframe, and now you have the first rung on the revenue ladder. If you want to use that as a base to raise $300,000 in capital, you now have the foundation on which to build this process.

I closed our first $600,000 in sales for x27 while living in my mom's basement... you can do this from anywhere.

You don't need to spend money on advertising. You can do this for free. You can build a list of emails for absolutely nothing, or hire somebody online for cheap. Put your processes in place, send your emails, book your meetings, and you can rapidly have a business in place that you can scale to as large as you want it.

It really is that simple. But you do have to get the process right. So in the next chapter, we're going to discuss exactly how to structure your cold email and cold calling operation.

CHAPTER 2.

My Dad Was
The Cold Call King

My dad was one of those people who invented something great out of nothing! He invented colored latex gloves. There was a shortage in the 1980s for one simple reason — doctors were not legally required to wear gloves before certain legislation had been introduced. Anyway, after AIDS and the HIV virus started; suddenly hygiene was deemed more important! When this law changed, suddenly there was a massive market for gloves, which basically emerged overnight.

And my dad saw an opportunity. He was an innovator, so he visited a balloon factory, and asked them to make latex gloves from their usual balloon products. After some pushback, they agreed to try and this was the catalyst for his entire multi-million-dollar business. He sold an absolute ton of these products. His team would cold call dentists, or anyone he thought might be interested in this product. So I had a first-hand demonstration of the power of cold calling from a very young age, even before I was born! You could say that selling was in my DNA!

If we fast forward to the present day, cold calling still works. It's still an effective strategy, and it's still a powerful weapon in any arsenal. x27 booked 3 meetings for a client in 24 hours with cold calling last week. But it needs to be rebooted. It needs a Jurassic World style reboot! I know most of you forgot about this movie, but in the late 2010s, Hollywood went through a phase of doing the 'soft reboot'. They'd take an old and beloved movie, boil it down to just the skeleton, and build a brand new movie on top of it. I want to do the same thing for your cold calling practice — if you have one. Let's break cold calling down to its skeleton, and then I'll show you a system that still works as well today as cold calling did in 1993.

SORRY DAD. THE COLD CALLING KING IS OUT. I'M THE COLD EMAIL KING.

Cold Email is all about taking the concepts that made cold calling effective 30 years ago, and then repeating them for a contemporary audience. Because the world has changed phenomenally over those 30 years. In 1991, Internet commerce barely existed, and social media didn't exist at all. Email was in its infancy, whereas today an email inbox might receive 500 messages every single day.

The cold calling environment is also completely different. It's far more likely that calls will be blocked automatically, or sent directly to spam. In short, it's harder to get your foot in the door.

But we still need meetings...

So that's why we need to reboot the way that we approach setting meetings. We need to develop a system that actually works for getting high level meetings, that doesn't kill the confidence of your team, and actually makes you sales.

Because, outbound, if we do it well, can be an extremely powerful tool. It's not that cold calls don't work, it's that the way we deal with the process needs to be restructured and refined. We need to identify and implement a strategy that works just as well today as my dad's approach worked in the 90s. And, luckily, a personalized cold email works — in some cases even better than cold calling worked in the 90s.

EVOLVING COLD CALLING

So cold calling still works. It's just not as effective. But I have had my own victories with cold calling, just to demonstrate that it can still deliver results. For example, there is a video of me on YouTube cold calling the director of marketing at Coca-Cola. In order to get through to him, I called the customer service desk and was transferred to another department, which then eventually transferred me to him. He picked up the phone, and I was able to begin pitching immediately, demonstrating that cold calling still works.

So I can do this... I cold called full time for a funded startup in New York City, made thousands of calls, yada yada yada.

It's just that cold calling is not as useful as it used to be! There are a ton of reasons for this, but the primary one is simply that cold emailing is more efficient and effective. Instead of cold calling Coca-Cola, which might have been one out of 100 calls that even connected that day, I can instead email 100 similar companies, and book 4 to 8 meetings in a few hours. That's why the traditional approach to cold calling is effectively dead. It's completely ineffective compared to this new strategy of cold email.

You can start making a list right now. Trust me, nothing is stopping you! You can pitch directly to these companies, and book meetings within a matter of hours. We've done this. We've booked meetings with Adidas, Morgan Stanley, Dunkin' Donuts, and hundreds of other brand-name companies, simply by sending customized cold emails. People are far more receptive to this approach, if only because nobody likes getting cold called.

Cold emails are significantly less intrusive. They are not a nuisance, which is another reason that they work so much better than cold calling. The person that you are contacting is already at his or her desk, they have the task in hand to check their email, and your email is simply one of many. All you have to focus on is ensuring that you get into their inbox in the first place, and that your message is compelling.

By sending cold email, you're effectively plugging into their everyday work journey. You're not spamming them, you're not annoying them, you're sending them something that they actually need. You've researched the company, you're offering them value, and if you communicate this to them effectively then they will recognise this immediately. That's how you book meetings. Effectively. You're offering them a treat; something for nothing. A tasty meal that requires no effort to cook or consume!

As an example, let's say the director of marketing for Coca-Cola is concerned about their social media team. It might not be delivering the sort of growth that the brand requires. Suddenly, your email pops into their inbox. Maybe this guy is talking to the director of HR, and they need somebody ASAP. Your email instantly provides value to him. He needs to hire somebody in order to achieve something and there you are! You can close that deal extremely quickly.

Cold email is therefore a strategy that gets you noticed right away. It is super-efficient. It can also be scaled so much more effectively than cold calling. It's more instant. It costs less. You can tweak the numbers and parameters easily. It just makes sense!

COLD EMAIL CASE STUDY

Using this effective cold call reboot strategy, we were able to book $600,000 in annual revenue in our first 30 days at x27.

But let me take you back to my parents' basement. How did I escape this undesirable situation?! And how did we get to this figure of $600,000 in recurring revenue for our agency in such a short period of time? You guessed it — emails, emails, emails!

So here is what worked for us. First, we crafted the offer that we would present to clients. I was an experienced agency worker at this point, living and working in New York City. And I'd already proved to myself I could be successful in sales, as I was working as the Director of Marketing for a $6 million agency; one of the top mid-level agencies in New York.

So I understood how to grow an agency via marketing. I knew I could deliver the work. And my offer actually reflected my own experience. I had the idea of simply telling the other agencies in the United States what I had already done, how I had generated an additional million in revenue for this already successful company. Using methods that I'd established, I was able to boost the sales of this agency by 16% and I just wanted to spread the word.

And the founder of the agency, who had become a friend and mentor of mine at that point, made an amazing video for us once we made them all that money. So I had a strong case study and a unique way of demonstrating it to potential clients. All that was left now was to directly email the agencies that we were targeting.

This was a straightforward process. All I did was sit in my parents' basement and start sending out emails. From the first batch of 20 emails that I wrote, I was able to arrange 8 meetings. And then the next day I sent another 20 emails, and 4 more meetings were arranged. And then on the third day, another 20 emails went out, and I managed to book in 6 more meetings. So that was nearly 20 meetings booked from just three days of work, and only 60 initial emails.

Once we connected with these clients, we told them about our agency, and the way that we worked. Now you can't expect everything to go well with every client. But if you have a plan in place, you will close on a good percentage of sales calls. Our marketing strategy was to charge $1,000 for the first sale, and then doubling this to $2,000, then $4,000, and eventually $8,000. After a while, we settled on $12,000 as the figure for our marketing plans.

People bought pretty quickly once they witnessed our value proposition. So I would sit there at the start of the day, send out my emails, make my sales calls, and literally wait for the money to begin rolling in! I would drive to Starbucks before beginning, get a caffeine hit, and then just fire away! I also remember playing Banjo Kazooie, the N64 game repeatedly, trying to speed run it for the nostalgia kick. And meanwhile, our bank account was stacking up with deals from cold email, to the point where we closed $600,000 in annual recurring revenue. In 60 days, we'd built a sustainable and high revenue marketing agency, using this cold email system.

Once we had this foundation in place, we were able to hire a sales team, and we grew rapidly because we had that consistent base. We hired a production team to fulfill the orders, and we rapidly ramped up our revenue to seven figures and beyond. And that was all on the back of these cold emails.

By now we were concentrating solely on marketing, as we had an effective system in place to generate clients and revenue. And we were ultimately able to generate over $100 million in leads across the agencies that we put in place, via the effective implementation of these cold emails. Once we'd reached this point, some of the big boys began to sit up and take notice. Silicon Valley companies that we'd been contacting became interested in our operation, and we were soon doing consulting for them as well.

The whole thing just snowballed on the strength of this cold email proposition. Because it is unbelievably effective if you get it right.

A JURASSIC WORLD STYLE REBOOT

In this chapter, I want to make it clear that cold calling has changed. That's why I'm referring to this new approach as Cold Email and the old system as Cold Calling Classic.

I've witnessed the Cold Calling Classic strategy first-hand, as I've worked in a call center. In this environment, the automatic dialer would ultimately contact countless people, until somebody answered, and you would then be connected to someone. And you knew absolutely nothing about this person whatsoever! You have no background, you have no insight into who they are, and you definitely have no clue whether or not they will be interested in buying. Based on that you may not be surprised to learn that this is not a particularly effective system!

On the other hand, Cold Calling Reboot is based on the exact opposite premise. It is about choosing your clients effectively, and ensuring that you don't need to reach out to thousands of uninterested parties. You will be contacting 50 people that you believe will buy and will be interested in your services, and conducting customized research in order to build what I refer to as the 'custom first line'. This is essentially a compliment, something like: "Hey, Mark, I love what you guys at Sony are doing with the PlayStation 5". Something specific that demonstrates that you understand what the company is involved with. And you don't need to invest a huge amount of research in acquiring this information; it is usually no more complicated than accessing the company website.

Once you've done this, you're ready to send the emails and book meetings, while you also have something of note to discuss during the calls. You know something about the client before you begin, which is hugely advantageous over going in completely cold. It may be cold calling from the client's perspective, but you are not entirely cold in the process, and this makes a massive difference. Hopefully, you will have also built a bit of rapport via email, and have enjoyed some favorable communication with them.

This helps you jump in a lot faster, and close better deals, as opposed to smiling and dialing randomly Wolf of Wall Street Style.

So what sort of business works best for this approach? Essentially, this is a B2B strategy. You're selling a product or service to other businesses. If you're directly targeting consumers, trying to sell the latest iPhone game to millions of people, this is not the ideal strategy for you. This approach is based on selling high ticket items to companies that can afford to pay. And that means anything from lead generation and marketing services, detailed DevOps projects, to back-end coding projects, and including specialized services — anything from copywriting to videography. Coding projects, app design, development, any sort of service that can benefit a big business.

Aside from big-ticket items, another approach that I've seen work with clients is to sell business loans via this system. You're pitching a large sum of money, so this approach works well in the credit space. The important thing is that you're making thousands of dollars from each sale, ideally more than $2,000, and that you're selling to other businesses directly. If you get the cold email and Cold Calling Reboot strategy in place, I promise you the sky is the limit.

BUILDING YOUR TEAM

Since I've been working in sales, I've become a huge fan of segmentation. This is something that you see in many business niches, and it also works in cold calling and cold email.

Each of the multiple parts that make up an agency can be broken down into individual roles. For example, sales comprise more than one process — there is email outreach, cold calling, research, taking the meeting, negotiating, signing the contract, and then passing it off to the production team to process. This means that sales are best served in two parts; you need somebody to send the emails and somebody else working on calls. You might even have a third person making the appointments and managing your calendar.

There is a simple reason for this approach. Let's say you hire a salesperson that is fantastic at closing deals — do you really want this person to spend four hours a day doing lead research, or sending custom first line emails? Obviously not! You want them on the phone as much as possible. That's why this segmentation into ideal roles works so effectively.

You might also find that there are people who are great at dealing with the detail of identifying leads, writing the custom first lines — which remember are compliments that drastically increase your conversion rate — and sending out emails. So get those guys to do that! This will ensure that your best salespeople are on the phone consistently. As you grow, this is an approach that can be steadily scaled, so that you have a three-pronged team. The sales team, the lead generation team, and the email sending team. And, of course, it's worth pointing out that they will grow as they specialize in a certain area. They'll get better the more they do, rather than having to spread themselves thinly over several tasks.

CASE STUDY – MAGENTO AGENCY

A little while back, my friend Alex, a different Alex than me, and his father were running a Magento agency. For the uninitiated, Magento is basically WordPress for nerds! It's a website builder that requires an entire development team to even set it up!

And they were selling this back when there was a migration from the first version of Magento to Magento 2.0. This was just supposed to be a button upgrade and relatively straightforward to install. But as is so often the case in technology and software, it wasn't quite as simple as the developers made it sound! So Alex and his father thought that this would be an ideal time to sell some websites, offering expertise to companies attempting to deal with this complex process.

But before Alex began this enterprise, I sat down with him and finalized all the details. We drilled into the key aspects of the operation. What is the typical process? How are you going to sell more to current customers? Will you be writing newsletter blasts? Are you cold calling? How much do you know about the customers when you contact them? And what do you say to customers when you finally speak to them?

We got all of this information together, decided to focus first on his clients before going cold, and then we worked on an email following the process that I described previously. Every single customer that we contacted received an email from us that had a custom first line, and a value proposition for the client. Something like this:

> Subject: Quick Question
> Hey, Dan, long time no speak, love how your business has been growing the last couple years, I like that you're still using our designs, they look great!
>
> Just noticed your site is still using Magento 1. If you haven't heard, Magento is removing support for all sites built in Magento 1 very soon, including the Acme Inc. site. This means your website will be unsupported and vulnerable to cybersecurity attacks.
>
> We have an upgrade package that we're implementing for a few of our ecommerce clients and would love to get you a new faster site built natively in Magento 2 to make sure your site stays secure and up to date with their support and improvements.
>
> Mind if I send over a few times to chat?
>
> —Alex

We promptly sent the information out to four of his best clients. And within weeks, Alex closed $100,000 in sales.

Two of them closed without even getting on the phone. That's the power of a solid offer and a warm cold email.

Imagine making an extra $100,000 next week, and generating this from your existing customers. That's the great thing about this system. It's not just about targeting new clients, it's also about generating increased revenue from existing customers. It's a powerful approach to sales that can be repeated over and over again. It can be used to target both clients that are already sold on your value proposition, and anyone that you believe may benefit from your products or services.

So now we've fully explained the rationale behind this system. You are entirely clear on why Cold Calling Reboot — replacing your current marketing strategy with a targeted multi-touch omni channel cold email campaign — is superior. And you also understand why cold email works. So now it's time to get into the actual process of doing it, and break down some of the finer points involved.

GIVING WITHOUT EXPECTATION

Would you help a complete stranger if it didn't cost money and you didn't get any credit?

If you answered yes, I quickly want to ask you to help somebody who's either just like you or like you were a couple years ago… not much experience, wanting to help humanity, looking for information but not sure where to find great material.

This is where you come in.

The only way that Robert and I can succeed in our mission to help entrepreneurs and sales teams is by reaching them. And most people judge books by their covers… and their reviews.

So, if you've found this book valuable so far, would you please take a moment right now and leave an honest review of this book and its content? It'll take you less than 30 seconds and your review will help one more salesperson hit their quota, one more entrepreneur support their family, and change one more life for the better.

To make that happen, all you have to do, and this will take less than 30 seconds, is leave a review.

If you're on Amazon, then leave a couple sentences about the book with a star rating.

Thanks for helping. It means a lot. You're about to crush with what we're going to go over in the next few chapters. You're gonna love this!

CHAPTER 3.

Making Cold Email Work

⬛

Cold calling is dead. We've established that.

Instead, we are warm calling. When we get customers on the phone, they've already opted in. And the best way to achieve this is via cold email.

So in this chapter, we're going through the entire Cold Email process. We're going to show you how to generate leads, what to write in your emails, everything that you need to know to execute a campaign that fills your calendar with meetings. So you never need to cold call ever again.

Sounds great, right? So let's get on with it!

SPECIFIC OFFERS

First things first, I want to tell you the most important aspect of all cold email campaigns. You must have a very specific offer. You must have something nailed down that you know that you can deliver. And that you know is attractive to a specific market. It can be a product or it can be a service, but it must be a compelling proposition.

And let me repeat…it must be specific! "We do web design" is useless! You need something that solves a problem for a specific group of people. This is why you don't go in cold in the first place. If you have the process honed before you begin then you can write basically anything in your cold email, and still get responses.

Instead of offering Web Design, offer Magento 2 migrations. Or instead of App Development, say you specialize in building connectivity apps for Universities.

That's how specific you want to get.

Of course, we're going to walk through how to write excellent cold emails, but you can write crap cold emails and still get responses if you pitch something people actually want to buy!

An example of this is when we did mobile app development, we were working with a university in Oklahoma. While we were talking to them, we discovered that their information technology program was actually split across six different teams — one would work with students, one with the faculty, one with admissions, and so on. Immediately when we heard this, we decided that we wanted to integrate the whole operation.

So we made them an offer. We'll rebuild your entire IT infrastructure and make your service more efficient. And we will ensure higher quality and increase security across all of your teams. We pitched, and they signed up to a six-figure contract to get going, which eventually became a $1 million per year tech retainer for us. It all comes down to identifying a need and then delivering something that addresses that need. Make it a no-brainer.

When it comes to writing your email, one of the first things to address is distinguishing yourself from the hundreds of other cold emails your potential customer gets daily. How do you create an offer that stands out from the crowd? It all comes down to the case study. This is the hardest and most important aspect of cold email, as it conveys exactly what you do. This is how you're going to sell your business to the client.

This case study will be the second line of your cold email template, with a custom compliment as your first line. The compliment is just a simple way to break the ice.

You're demonstrating that you know something about the client that you're targeting. The overall structure of a cold email will go something like this:

Hey John,

Heard about you while looking up Marketing Directors for major hospitals and love your backstory — incredible that you work as a volunteer firefighter as well.

I specialize in iOS development for the healthcare industry. Recently, we built an app for Johns Hopkins that has increased their patient happiness rating by 75% through an automated dashboard.

Interested in improving your patient happiness at Baylor? Let me know and I'll send over some times to chat.

Thanks,
Alex

That's an example of an email that will generate meetings because you're effectively separating yourself from your competitors. Are any of your competitors going direct to clients with a pitch like this? No! So you're right in front of the client immediately. These are busy people. They don't want to go away and research healthcare app development companies. They don't want to release an RFP and have other people pitch. They want the solution to arrive in front of them, as if by magic!

And this is exactly what you achieve by using this cold email strategy. You're offering these people a solution on a silver platter. Now they can make themselves look good to their bosses, and make it seem like they are the proactive ones! It's a win-win situation!

SUBJECT LINE

How do you get potential customers to open the email? You need a good subject line.

Luckily this is the easy part. We have a complete list of subject lines proven to perform later on in this book, but for now just use the subject line Quick Question. This subject line has consistently outperformed other subjects in our testing.

Test Quick Question in your campaigns and you'll be sure to get a high number of opens!

FRAMING THE COMPLIMENT

So let's talk about the compliment, and how we figured this out. First, there tend to be two camps when it comes to cold emails, and I've experienced both of them. The first is the 1,000 email a day spammer, who creates what they think is a perfect offer (but is usually an untested and un-spellchecked message) and then circulates it to as many clients as possible. I don't like or favor that approach, but I will concede that it can work with certain offers, like business loans or commodities.

Instead, for high ticket selling, customization is far more effective. Writing a handful of personalized emails, and making sure you only send to extremely relevant prospects, just works better.

In our approach to cold email, we have adopted the Pareto principle — ie. 80% of results come from 20% of the work. I don't think the pure spam game works for the majority of people, and I also know that you will experience more success with a handful of customized emails than a spammer will see in their entire (short) careers.

The best cold email is a fully custom written one, and the worst performing email is a generic template. But fully customized cold emails can take hours, so I realized that utilizing a customized first line would help to transfer the power of a fully personalized cold email while saving as much time as the spamming strategy. It's a hybrid approach that provides the best of both worlds. All it takes is one custom sentence, and suddenly your email has become far more likely to receive a response.

So we've established the case study and the compliment. The final part of the picture is the call to action. This is the least personalized and customized part of the email. In fact, it can pretty much be copied and pasted. But it does need to be asked in a specific form to prompt a "yes" or "no" answer. This is much more favorable than an open-ended question like: "what is your biggest problem at the moment?".

Keep things as simple as possible, and make things easy for these CEOs and CTOs. They're extremely busy people, with thousands of things going on at once.

Here are two ways to end your cold emails:

The basic:
Interested? Let me know and I can send over a few times to chat.

And the advanced:

Are you interested in {{benefit you provide}} for {{company name}}? Let me know and I can send over a few times to chat.

Example:

Can you take on more clients at Fuzz? Let me know and I can send over a few times to chat.

CREATING YOUR SALES TEAM

At this point, I'd like to talk about how you can restructure your sales team to achieve better results.

Most sales teams I've encountered have everyone doing everything — the sales director is closing deals, the junior sales people are running calls, everyone is writing their own proposals. It's a mess.

Instead, my approach is to break all of the tasks up into component parts, and then get people to specialize. This is a technique used by many successful companies, as it enables workers to practice a particular field repeatedly, and excel as a consequence. This leads to much better results. Imagine if your best closer only closed deals. How many more deals would get done? Or the best lead generator only did research. See where we're going with this? Once your team is specialized and doubling down on the tasks that they're best at, your company will skyrocket.

It's also important to have a CRM (customer resource management) software in place. This plays a key monitoring role in the whole process. This software will help your team track what's going on. Everything from where a client is in the process (have we sent a proposal yet?) to the tasks being completed by each person, can be tracked in a good CRM. Luckily, an entire industry of these tools has sprung up, and you can get started with anything from Zendesk to Salesforce and more. If you want my up to date recommendation, please go to **coldemailmanifesto. com/tools**

The important thing with a CRM system is to ensure that your entire sales team is connected. Your lead generator, first line writer, appointment setter and closer all need to be tracked by the system. And all of the data needs to be easily accessible, so that your sales director can manage all of the information. This is ultimately the person that reports back to you, so they need all of the data at their fingertips.

BENCHMARK STATS

Speaking of data, you need to pay attention to benchmark stats. There are certain targets that you should be aiming for, if you want to do cold email effectively.

First, your lead generator should be able to locate 200 leads every day. A lead includes: First Name, Last Name, Title, Company Name, Website and Email Address. Typically, this lead generator is located in a developing economy or Third World country, where there are fewer demands in terms of salary. And the great thing is that there are thousands of people that have been working on this over the last couple of decades, so you won't have to train them. If you find one that requires training, hire somebody else.

For your custom compliment writer, this is a little bit trickier, so I would suggest 3–5 minutes for each first line is a reasonable benchmark. And the cold email sender should achieve a meeting book rate between 4–8%. Next, your meeting booker should be able to basically fill your calendar with meetings. If you get this going effectively, you will be so busy that you won't have time to breathe!

And, finally, your sales closer should be getting between 10–25% close rate from cold leads, depending on the size of your deal and 80% for warm marketing qualified leads.

Job Title:	Lead Generator	First Line Writer	Cold Email Manager	Appointment Setter	Closer
Lead Measure:	200 relevant leads generated per day	200 First lines written per day	200 Emails sent per day 1 Campaign optimization per email batch sent	Up to 300 email responses per day	8 meetings per day
Lag Measure:	0% bounce rate	20% response rate	80% open rate	80% of Cold Email positive responses become meetings	25% close rate

If you can knock these numbers out regularly, you're good to go. You're going to be talking to lots of important people and valuable clients on a constant basis. Now there is always the possibility that you won't achieve the results that you're looking for immediately. In this scenario, because everyone has specialized roles, you can easily see where the system is breaking down! I would allow your team at least 90 days, and possibly as much as 180 days, before you reflect on where the process is going wrong.

But pay attention to what you can control (the lead measures in the chart above) and the results will come.

COLD EMAIL – THE PROCESS

So now we're clear on what your sales team is being measured against, let's go through exactly what you need to do step-by-step to ensure that cold email works at a high level.

EMAIL WARMUP

As more people started using cold email, and the spam rates increased, spam filters had to get stronger to fight against this deluge of spam.

This hurts everyone trying to sell via email.

The best way to get around that is to 'warm up' your inbox for a few weeks before sending emails.

These warm up tools will connect with each other and send automatically generated text back and forth, to trick the spam filters into seeing your new inbox as a real person.

They also automatically save your emails from the spam box if they happen to land in there.

For a list of my favorite email warmup tools, please go to **ColdEmailManifesto.com/tools**.

DOMAIN

You'll also want to sell from a domain that is not your main domain name. Why? Because you're new to this, and everyone makes mistakes.

Do you want every email you send from your main .com email address going to spam for the rest of your life? No.

So instead of sending from CompanyName.com, send from CompanyName.co or CompanyName.io or any other domain that forwards back to your main site.

TARGETING THE CUSTOMER

Now that your tools are set up, you need to be hyper-specific with your customer. You need to understand the person that is buying intimately. Are you selling to HR, or the CTO of a company? Are you delivering a hiring tool, or a tech solution? What is the size of the business that you're dealing with? Once you begin to answer these questions, you can create an impression of your client.

A strong customer profile will include the title of the person, the company size, and its revenue. Once this has been broken down, I typically target Golden Geese companies — those that are worth between $5–150 million annually. The reason for this is that they are big enough to be able to afford your product or service, but small enough that they won't drag you through an entire excruciating enterprise process!

The other important point is to drill down into the specifics of the industry that you're dealing with. For example, using the term Ecommerce to describe your industry is essentially completely meaningless. Every company is in Ecommerce! This is utterly useless information! Take fashion behemoth Alexander Wang. Do they sell products online as an ecommerce company? Yes… but instead, you might choose to describe Alexander Wang as a fashion company, which tells you something far more useful about what they do, and, importantly, how they describe themselves. Make sure you know exactly the type of customer you're reaching out to, understand how they would describe themselves, and where exactly they would derive value from your solution.

BUILDING YOUR TARGETS

The next part of the process is building your list of targets.

Imagine you're selling Twitter management. You might be searching for the Chief Marketing Officer of a company, which will be a Golden Goose company between $5–$150 million in revenue. Considering the service that you're providing, it is important to target people who aren't achieving their potential on Twitter. So you want a company with considerably less than 100,000 followers.

It might sound tricky to identify a company like this, but there is a simple solution. You go to a freelancing platform like Upwork. And you create a job indicating that you're looking for leads, while outlining the criteria that you're searching for. A ton of people that are both talented and experienced in this area will respond, and you can select someone appropriate to identify companies and CMOs.

Here's the exact job post to put up:

Job Post Title: Lead Generation List building

Hey! I need data for the following criteria.

Criteria:
Consumer companies in the US with between $5m–150m in revenue

Must have under 100,000 followers on their main twitter account

Need the following for each:
- First Name
- Last Name
- Title
- Email
- Company Name
- Website
- Twitter handle
- Number of followers

Budget $15 for complete data of 100 leads per criteria.

All email addresses must be verified by you before delivery.

Usually, I will start with a small group of three or four different lead generators. Hiring multiple freelancers to do the same job is the easiest way to screen applicants, plus you're paying them to interview with you!

And it's not just about the quantity of leads, you also need to be focused on the quality. The best way to begin achieving this is to run the leads through an email verifier. There are several of these programs available via a Google search. Simply Google "email verification" and you shouldn't have any problem whatsoever in locating a suitable service. To see my recommended email verification tool, please visit **ColdEmailManifesto.com/tools**.

At this point, you can check the bounce rate. If emails are being made up, your email verification tool should find them. If you send without verifying, you might see a bounce rate of 30–40%, and that would instantly send your account to the spam box — killing both your campaigns and your domain. You should be aiming for a bounce rate of no higher than 8%.

RUN OUTBOUND EMAIL CAMPAIGNS

You have the leads. You have the client profiles. Next, come the outbound email campaigns. Now we're going to use a subject line that has been around for nearly a decade. But it still works! If you use this subject line on the right leads, then you can expect 80–90% open rates. It's "Quick question". Something straightforward and easy to understand. No need to reinvent the wheel!

At this point, again we're using the example of companies that don't have a strong Twitter following.

So your email could be something like this:

Subject: Quick question
Hey Jason, big fan of Focusrite — I use your audio equipment every day for our podcast.

I specialize in growing Twitter accounts for consumer brands and noticed Focusrite has less than 100,000 followers on Twitter. We recently helped a consumer brand go from 20,000 to 100,000 followers in just seven days and would love to do the same for you.

Want more engaged followers on the Focusrite twitter? Let me know and I can send over a few times to chat.

Thanks,
Alex

Simple as that.

But that's just a little bit too simple, right?! Life is never that easy!

You're right. It's not enough to just send that single email. What I have found is that a lot of people won't respond to the first email. They might be too busy. It might hit them at 10 AM during a mandatory meeting, or they may prioritize other things. They might also just forget to respond! So following up on that initial email is extremely important. But I must also emphasize, particularly to avoid being marked as spam, that I don't recommend following up more than four times.

So three days after the first email, you haven't heard back from the client. At this point, you send a very simple follow-up.

NOTE: All of these follow-ups should be in the same thread as the previous email. No new subject line is needed.

4 Days Later:

Hey Jason, I'm sure you're busy and wanted to bump this up!

Okay, that might not work either! So now you move into the third email, which I describe as the 'big win' email. You tell them about another case study that you have, and you announce it to them as if it's a huge news item.

Hey Jason,
We just helped Sony break 100K on their God of War campaign! Would still love to help your Twitter grow.

Let me know and I can send over some times.

Thanks,
Alex

Then the final email can be described as a breakup email. And it will go with something like this:

Hey Jason,
At this point, I'll assume that growing Focusrite's Twitter account is not a priority for this year. Please let me know if that changes.

Thanks,
Alex

The reason that the breakup email works so well, is that most people in business are accustomed to having salespeople hound them mercilessly. This gives them a bit of breathing room and provides them with the opportunity to respond. It also gives the psychological impression that this opportunity is slipping away and that can be really compelling. So don't neglect this part of the process, even if you believe the client will never respond, as this last email works way more often than you think it should. Of course, you can't hook every fish, but always go through the process. Getting a solid "yes" or "no" is the goal — we don't want clients hanging out in limbo.

ARRANGING A MEETING

Okay... now you've been through the email process, and you've hopefully attracted a client. Next you need to arrange a meeting. For this, you should send a simple email, with a quick greeting and three bullet points of possible meeting times. You don't need any more than that, as you're going to connect with this person further on a potential call.

Before we break this down, I want to demonstrate that you can target clients beyond your wildest dreams, and that seem unreachable, via a simple cold email strategy.

One time we were working with a social media marketing company. They actually did the social media for a bunch of TV shows. They wanted us to connect them with some big TV production companies. And we managed to do this (although I can't name the broadcaster for legal reasons!).

Now anyone that has spent time in Los Angeles, where this company was located, knows that trying to break into this industry is a virtually impossible task. It really is like putting a message in a bottle and sending it out into the ocean! But we made it happen.

In order to meet with this company, we sent three emails and then we cold called them. After they responded we sent more emails, chased them down, and went through this entire chain of command. We started with the person who was in charge of marketing, moved on to the Director of Marketing on a specific show, then the show runners at some of the specific programs, and just kept following up continually. Eventually, one of the show runners did respond, and that was our point of entry. From there, we were able to pitch to them over email what we intended to do to promote their show, and this point of contact became our liaison.

Eventually, after a lot of back and forth, they managed to coordinate a meeting with eight people, including the heads of the network. So the top people at this TV station heard our direct social media pitch. That's a great example of how you might not break through with your first email, but that you sometimes have to be persistent. Work within the constraints of the company that you're targeting. If you have to talk to three people and coordinate calendars, do it. If you have to talk to two assistants, be ready to do that too.

If the money is good enough, and the size of the average project for this agency was $500,000, then it's worth pursuing it with determination. You won't win every time, but if you get a few wins of this nature it will make such a massive difference to your business and life.

ROCK SOLID APPOINTMENT SETTING SCRIPT

Once a prospect responds to your cold email, they will either have questions, or will want you to send times. Here's the script for when they reply positively:

> Great! How does Monday at 3pm EST work? Also available Wednesday at 10am or flexible on Thursday.
>
> Thanks,
> Alex

If the prospect has other questions like pricing or case studies. Respond like this:

> Hey! Happy to answer that in detail. How does Monday at 3pm EST work? Also available Wednesday at 10am or flexible on Thursday.
>
> Thanks,
> Alex

Note that just because a prospect asks a question does not mean you need to answer it in the email. The goal is to book calls, so ask for calls.

Then once you have a solid meeting arranged, you pass the process over to your salesperson.

THE SALES CALL

I can't emphasize enough that it's really important to get the tone of your proposal calls correct. When you're trying to sell to big businesses, there is a tendency to go in there with all guns blazing. Tell them how great you are, tell them how wonderful your product is, and tell them how much they need it. This approach may seem completely logical, but it is a big mistake.

Instead, I would view the proposal call as similar to a doctor's diagnosis. When you go to see a doctor, they don't immediately start pushing solutions on you, and tell you how great they will be for your health. They ask you questions, they discuss symptoms, they might run a couple of tests, and only then do they provide you with a potential solution.

And that's what we're doing here. We're not telling the company what the problem might be, we're finding out from them what their problem actually is, and then offering a solution to the problems that they have acknowledged. That is a much more powerful and effective approach. Of course, we already know what the solution is, but this discourse is a critical part of the process.

So when you're on a proposal call with a client, I would recommend the following structure. First, it's great to begin with a bit of banter, a little small talk, maybe chat about sports or where they live, possibly even family, for a little while. Simple rule here — no politics, no religion! The only exception to that rule is if you're 100% sure that you share political or religious views; if that's the case then definitely bring it up!

Then you move into the call. It's critically important at this stage, as I just mentioned, to ask some questions, and get some feedback from the client. Here are the actual discovery questions we wrote for an SEO agency.

Notice how highly specific they are to the service they offer. Yours should be just as specific to your offer.

Questions

- **Can you tell me more about your company and your role within the organization?**
  - » What's your main value proposition?
  - » Who are your ideal customers?
  - » What work do you personally oversee?
- **What areas of growth are you focusing on for (current year)?**
  - » What actions on the site are most important to you (white paper download, demo, free trial, etc.)?
  - » KPIs?
  - » Any dollar amounts you assign to these conversions?

- **What issues are you having with your organic search marketing strategy?**
- **When you responded to the email I sent, could you tell me about what came to mind when you thought about us working together?**
- **What would be a slam dunk?**
- **How much are you currently spending on SEO?**

These are just some examples, and you should customize them to sell whatever service you're working with. The important thing is that the questions guide the customer through the sales process. You are gently persuading them into buying, rather than pushing them forcefully.

One of the critical aspects is to identify a big problem that they experience, and then frame the product or service that you're selling as the solution. This means that it's valuable to ask them as many questions about the problem as possible:

Have they tried to solve it in the past?

If they did try to solve it, why did this fail?

If they haven't tried to solve it, why not?

What is going on in the organization to stop them from attempting to solve something that they've identified as a big problem?

And then once you've gathered all of this information, you should talk about your case studies and past work in your answers. For example, a company might reveal a certain issue, and you can tell them that you were just talking with the CEO of another major apparel company about the same issue and once you addressed the problem, they experienced a vast improvement in their performance. By answering in this way you're demonstrating to the client that you can offer them value.

Another important thing to note is that you're being affirmative with the client. You're telling them that they are correct, and that you've experienced this previously in the past. And you're then offering them the solution to the problem that they have expressed.

CLOSE THE DEAL

Now comes an extremely important part of the process. Closing the deal.

First, you ask a closing question:

Are you guys ready to get started?

At this point, you pass the baton to the proposal team and ask them to write a beautiful proposal that sells the company. You can see the entire proposal we use to close deals for services businesses at **ColdEmailManifesto. com/proposal** I'd share it here but it would make this book about 10% longer, just go to the website.

Deliverables are all important here. The proposal begins with an executive summary that talks about everything you discussed during the call. Then you talk about what you're going to do for them and express the timeline involved with achieving this. Finally, you need to outline pricing and cost structure.

I like to take 50% of the project's cost upfront and then take the final payment over time based on dates and not deliverables.

Sign the contract and Boom! Then you move on to the next of the 9 other meetings that you have booked for that day, as you're continually following the process that we've outlined already.

PAYING YOUR TEAM

Now your machine is humming. You have your team in place, and you're beginning to book meetings and attract clients. Let's get down to brass tacks… how much should you pay your team?

This is a question that I get asked all the time. How do you appropriately compensate the people working in your business? So let's break it down.

For the lead generators, you're usually hiring someone from a developing economy or Third World country, and you should be paying them around 10–25 cents per lead. For first line writers, you will either pay them hourly, possibly around $15 per hour, or you can even pay per first line, which would be $0.50–$1 per line.

For your cold email campaign senders and managers, you need to be paying them a monthly salary. Somewhere between $2,000 and $4,000 every month. You can afford to be flexible here, and allow these people to do the job part-time. The important thing is to get good people in place. Also, if you decide to break the appointments into a separate role, you can pay less for your cold email senders.

For the appointment setters, I would tend to pay per appointment. $5–10 per meeting that they get booked on the calendar. But this only applies if they're just handling inbound leads from cold emailing.

Someone working in a more holistic role will require a monthly salary, and that would usually be around $3,000 at present market rates in the United States.

You could also possibly pay them a 1% commission on net revenue if you feel that they're doing outstanding work for you.

The closer is a more senior role, and can have a base of around $5,000 with a 3–5% commission, or if it's a commission-only closer, they will be happy with 10%.

A commission structure can be part of your overall pay structure, and the closers will receive a bigger slice as they're doing the heavy lifting.

So 3–5% commission goes to the closer, with the margins depending on your business. By paying these amounts to your sales team, you will still have plenty of profit as a business owner.

THE IMPORTANCE OF THE CLAWBACK

You want your operation to be honest and authentic, and for your salespeople to be pitching value propositions that you can actually deliver. A useful way that I found to achieve this is to compensate salespeople on a monthly basis, as long as the client sticks around. You don't want to be handing out a year's worth of commission to a salesperson, because what will happen is that they will begin lying and promising things that they can't deliver. They won't care about this, though. Because they will still get paid even if the client leaves!

Put in place a clawback, which means that if a client leaves then a salesperson loses the commission. That means that your operations team and salespeople are going to be on the same page, with the salespeople really wanting the client to succeed with the product or service.

CHAPTER 4.

The Pre-Work

Not everybody is ready to send cold emails right away. So, let's make sure you're ready.

One of the biggest issues I've encountered with cold email is that companies will attempt to do it without having the fundamentals in place. You need to have everything nailed down, otherwise cold email won't work correctly. And then you won't get the results you want, and you might end up dismissing cold email forever. Or concluding that cold email is just spam, or that it's ineffective. Which would be a terrible waste.

The reason this happens is that companies are missing three key components of a winning cold email offer. Those three components are case studies, the offer itself, and the target market.

And in this chapter, we're going to take you through those three key components step-by-step. Be ready! Each section has homework to help you build an effective campaign.

CASE STUDIES

First, you need to get your case studies super-aligned. You want to put an offer in place that is a no-brainer for potential clients. And the important component is that you want the target market to be someone that can afford your offer. The reason for this is that cold email is different from inbound; you're essentially driving the process. So you need to do 90% of the work and pitch an offer, not a service. I'll give you an example.

An agency will compose a cold email, and it will say something like the following:

Subject: Quick Question
Hey Mark,
Are you looking to do any web development projects?

We specialize in all languages and can design sites or apps as well.

Let me know what you think.

Regards,
Carl

This email is trash.

Why? That's pitching a service, not pitching an offer.

Pitching an offer is about producing something that a customer can buy. For example:

Subject: Quick Question

Hey Karen, huge fan of the work you're doing with Acme tours — loved the last video!

I specialize in writing emails for tour companies. Recently, one client increased their sales by 141% with just one newsletter.

I'd love to do the same for you. Is that something you'd be interested in?

Thanks,
Mark

That's the way any company doing cold emails should pitch. Instead of telling the client that they do copywriting, tell them specifically who you work with as a copywriting firm, tell them that you have achieved outstanding results, and then offer to do the same for them.

Here's an example from the world of app development:

Subject: Quick Question

Hey Brian, sunny skies again in Boca Raton — huge fan of the city!

We just wrapped up a new project with the city of San Diego Treasury Department where we built a custom application that calculated how much tax is due to the city, with a back-office system that enables Treasury offices to collect taxes more efficiently.

Would love to discuss rewriting your tax collection software, to help streamline your processes and add new features.

Would this interest you? Drop me a line and we can arrange a call at your convenience.

Regards,
Jennifer

Again, that's selling a specific offer to build custom tax collection software for city Treasury departments. This is just an example; the company could pitch any *specific* app development or technology product, but they can't pitch *any* app development or technology product.

Another example could be a company that is selling pay-per-click ads; a huge market. Their email might go something like this:

Subject: Quick Question
Hi Samia, love all the work you're doing for Acme Residential, congrats on 6 years!

Been running Google ads for 12 years and have filled over 11,000 beds for rehab facilities across the country.

Would love to do the same for you. Let's talk?

Thanks,
Winston

Another specific pitch — offering a service that has been outlined clearly. Finally, let's look at an example of social media marketing:

Subject: Quick Question
Hey Roger, congrats on winning the best in Las Vegas award! Figured you'd like this:

I've grown dozens of Instagram accounts for realtors over the last few years and specialize in finding new customers, not building followers.

Would love to do the same for you. Let's talk?

Thanks,
Chris

Notice how specific these offers are. We aren't selling "social media", we sell "Instagram growth for lawyers." It's not "web & mobile design", it's "tax collection software for City Treasury Departments." The point is that you need to squeeze your case studies into one sentence pitches in order to get ready for sending cold emails. And make them hyper-specific. It's not enough to just target a specific industry, they also need to solve a specific problem. Ideally, your pitch is also something that has increased revenue for businesses previously, so that you can cite this in your email. Remember, sugar, salt and fat. We're like McDonald's. Deliver that value by promising to make them money, the same way McDonald's promises to make you feel good by giving you sugar, salt and fat!

One important point to understand is that your case study must appeal to companies that are similar to the ones that you sold to previously. So the previous sale that you cited in your case study can't be too specific. I know that I've just stated that it must be specific — but it must also be generalizable to the rest of the market. You have to be specific enough that somebody in that market will immediately resonate with the benefits, but general enough that it can be applied to a decent number of companies.

Look at the above email scripts again if you need to — they're the perfect balance of being specific to an industry, but also being buyable by more than one company.

And I'd like to emphasize again that targeting an appropriate niche is important. I mentioned 'Golden Geese' companies previously — this is a concept that needs to be engraved in your brain! Any company generating between $5 million and $150 million in revenue. I find that companies in this niche have the ability to pay, and aren't ground down by layers of management and decision-making that can be associated with massive enterprises.

Companies at this level will be willing to spend $50,000 on a project and approve it in a few days. A mom and pop store might approve a project in a few days, but only pay you $200. And an enterprise may be willing to pay you $50,000, or even more, but it might take six months to approve the project.

So you want to ensure that your target market fits with the criteria of desperately requiring your services, while also being able to afford them.

You can derive your target market from existing case studies. If you've done a great job for a major hospital in the past, you can now sell to other major hospitals. If a nonprofit has purchased a logo that you produced, you can now target other nonprofits. And so on.

Finally, if you have no case studies, you might not be quite ready for cold email just yet. That's the cold, hard reality. However, if you are starting from scratch then it is possible to borrow case studies from other agencies. This requires you to cold call an existing agency and ask to become a partner. We've actually covered this in our 'Email10k' course — you can check out all our courses at **ColdEmailManifesto.com/courses**

HOMEWORK

Review your case studies and select three to use in your cold email campaigns.

A GOOD OFFER

A good offer is specific and is tied to a monetary goal. This means that somebody hearing your offer for the first time will immediately know that it's going to make them more money, or help them look good in their job. Ideally, money is better, because if you think about what McDonald's does — it's by no means the best fast food in the world, but they give you sugar, salt and fat! And making someone more money is the sugar, salt and fat of the enterprise world. If you can provide that to someone, it's incredibly easy to sell.

With this in mind, I try to reframe everything that we offer in terms of how much money it's going to make our potential clients. If you're designing logos, you're going to help increase brand credibility, which will, in turn, lead to more sales. If you are building a website, you're either going to increase overall customer satisfaction, or conversion rate, which will lead to more sales. If you're copywriting, rather than just churning out prose, you're writing newsletter blasts or creating blogs that will lead directly to more sales.

This will allow you to create a no-brainer offer. Something so valuable to the company that they would be stupid to decline. And they believe you because you can demonstrate that you succeeded in the past. An excellent example of a no-brainer offer would be:

I will write three newsletters and if you don't make more money than you spent hiring me, I'll give you the money back.

ANOTHER GOOD NO-BRAINER OFFER:

I will review all of your Facebook ad campaigns, and if we don't find at least two optimizations that make you more money then you don't have to work with us any longer. But if we do find them, let's scale your ads.

MORE EXAMPLES OF NO-BRAINER OFFERS:

Facebook ads — Manage ads for 30 days, if no return on investment, we refund our fee.

Newsletter copywriting — Write 3 newsletters for 50% commission, no sales, no payment.

Lead generation (Outbound) — Book 10 meetings in 4 weeks or your money back.

Website design — Wireframes only, if you don't like where this is headed, we give you your money back.

Mobile app development — Wireframes only, if you don't like where this is headed, you get your money back.

Backend development — A two-hour tech review, we can end the contract after that if you don't see the value.

Branding — Let's just do the mood board, if you don't like where this is headed, we can refund.

Search Engine Optimization — In-depth review (not the sort that other people give for free) if you don't like it, we'll refund.

DOMAIN NAME

Okay, we've got the case study and offer drilled down. Now we need to select a domain name.

Now I know exactly what you're thinking. "We've already got a domain name, and it's a perfect fit for our business! We don't need a new domain name! Why on earth would we need to consider this?!"

That's a perfectly valid observation, but there is a reason! You already use your existing domain name to interface with the rest of the world. The most obvious example of this would be Google.com, which is obviously known by virtually everyone in the world. That brand is extremely important to Google, and so they don't want to do anything that will ever harm it.

On a smaller scale — although you might reach the revenue of Google eventually, anything can happen — that applies to you as well. You need to protect your domain name and online identity as if your life depends on it. In some cases, your life will depend on it!

One potential issue with cold email is that it can be marked as spam, and potentially cause problems for your established domain.

Again, you're probably thinking right now... I thought that we weren't spamming?! Sure, but when you start with cold email, just like any new skill, you will inevitably make mistakes. If you think that you're going to walk into cold email and get everything 100% correct immediately, that's not beyond the realm of possibility, but it is not likely to happen.

But there is a simple solution to this problem. You just buy domain names that are similar to your existing domain. Because if you send out, for example, 3,000 cold emails on a whim, and end up being marked as spam, that will be it for your domain. This could be a total calamity for your business, particularly if it is reasonably well-established. Think: internal company emails hitting the spam box, invoices to customers not getting through, etc. Protect your main domain name like the golden banner it is.

The best way to get around this potential pitfall is by using similar domains. We've provided tools that we recommend to assist with this process at **coldemailmanifesto.com/tools**. But let me give an example of what you might need to purchase. Our main domain is **X27marketing.com**. And we also own **X27.io**, **X27marketing.co**, **experiment27.com** — we've got a ton of these! And you'll have a separate email inbox for every domain name that you're using. I would recommend buying only one to begin your initial campaign, but you can ramp this up as you expand your operation.

So your homework for this module is to buy up several domain names that are similar to your current domain name, and redirect them back to your existing sites. Redirecting is not particularly difficult to do; search for this on Google. It's worth mentioning that loads of really big companies have done this, even changing their main domain in certain circumstances. Everybody does this! It's the norm for companies to sell from non-standard domain names, so make sure that you follow this process.

HOMEWORK:

Buy three similar domain names and redirect them back to your main site

EMAIL SIGNATURE

In later chapters of this book, I'm going to talk about crafting the perfect cold email. But before you can do this, you need to calibrate your inbox effectively. And that means setting up the signature as well. This is really important. In case you don't know, the signature is the bottom section of your cold email. It seems fairly innocuous, but it's something that most people get wrong.

Email signatures that have giant images, or a bunch of different text, or 20 different links to disparate aspects of your company hurt you more than help you. These are all approaches that you must avoid. A good email signature will simply have your name, contact details, and one strong link. Clean, straightforward and impactful.

Here's mine:

—

Alex Berman | *Founder*
EXPERIMENT 27
12249 Fake Road Rd, Orlago, FL 34711
Mobile: 321 555 3123
alex@x27marketing.com | x27marketing.com

Another important thing to understand is that images lead to higher manual spam complaints, so the fewer images that you have in your email the better. Providing an avatar or image of yourself can also harm your cold email in many cases. "Why?" I hear you ask! Maybe you look too much like a model. Maybe you don't look enough like a model (many of us have this problem)! Or maybe the person that you're sending the email to has some pre-conceived prejudices, of which even they are not aware. The point is that it can only hurt to include your picture. You're gaining nothing and potentially losing quite a lot. Equally, by providing images and links we're encouraging people to click around our website, when we want them to book a meeting and buy our product or service. So, again, they add very little value, or potentially detract from the aim of the exercise.

There is a general template that you can follow for your signature.

- First line: First name, last name, title.
- Second line: Company name.
- Third line: Office address.
- Fourth line: Best phone number.
- Fifth line: Email and website.

HOMEWORK:

Set that email signature up right now and add it to your email.

SETTING UP THE INBOX AND AUTHENTICATING

But you're still not ready to send cold emails just yet! You need to set up your inbox correctly.

This is more important than it might sound. Spam filters are becoming ever more sophisticated, so failing to calibrate your inbox correctly is the easiest way to get marked as spam. And this will render the whole operation completely pointless, or even damaging. So you do need to ensure that you set your email inbox up in the right way.

Firstly, you must fill out the complete information included in the account setup. This means ensuring that you have a profile picture, and that your first name, last name and address are all provided. Also, make sure that you set up everything inside of your G Suite. Because Google automatically checks all of this. If it's not properly filled out, it will count against you.

The next part of the process is to authenticate your email. Before I explain this, I just want to give a quick warning. This could conceivably change in the future. I tried to ensure that everything in this book is completely future-proofed, but this is one example of something valuable now that could evolve in years to come.

DMARC is a system that has been created to help you send emails at scale without being marked as spam. It's a verification system that Google and several other major providers use. It's not a license to spam anybody and everybody, but it has been designed to provide receivers with better judgment regarding domain reputations. DMARC provides a platform that enables the sender to publish policies that protect against spam and phishing, effectively building domain reputations.

This is a little technical, but DMARC is the equivalent of SSL for a website. It's an identifier that gives credence to a certain email platform. SSL is linked to the https precursor that I'm sure everyone listening to this book has encountered on the Internet. This system ensures that nefarious people cannot just set up fraudulent domains online, and have them accepted as being legitimate. Https results in a verification mark in the top left-hand corner of your browser, which identifies pages as being secure. DMARC essentially does the same job for email.

But the best way going forward is to Google "how to add DMARC". That way any information that you locate will always be up-to-date.

HOMEWORK:

Add DMARC to your domain.

WARMING UP THE EMAIL

The final task in this chapter is to warm up your email inbox. If you've followed everything so far, you will have set up your email account, your signature will be calibrated, and you've sorted out DMARC so that you're not identified as spam. So, finally, in order to actually avoid the spam box, Google needs to believe that you're real. You know that you're real, but Google can still conclude that you're not real!

What that means is that new users shouldn't sign up for a service, and immediately begin sending thousands of emails without receiving replies. That's a cast-iron way to get marked as spam immediately. Spam filters will tag you as a spammer instantly, nobody will ever see your emails, and then you have to go through the whole process of setting up a new email inbox. Which I'm sure you want to avoid!

Luckily, there are automated tools that will warm up your inbox for you. There are several of these available at **coldemailmanifesto.com/tools**. These plug your email into a web of other email inboxes, which then continually send messages back and forth. It will also generate text, which will demonstrate to Google that you're not a spammy inbox. It serves the purpose of warming up your domain, ensuring that your cold emails end up in the Primary inbox and not in Spam or Promotions. This can be done manually, but I would certainly recommend utilizing tools, as this will simply make the process more convenient and quicker.

HOMEWORK:

Sign up for an Email Warmup tool and hit Go!

That's everything you need to know about preparing yourself to send cold emails. In the next chapter, we're going to address lead generation. So that you can build lists of people to contact!

CHAPTER 5.

Lead Generation

At this point, you've done a lot of prep. You've gone through the pre-work, you have your case studies in-place, you know where you're positioning yourself in the market, you know who you're targeting. And your mindset should be in the right space to start taking advantage of cold email.

But before you go any further, we need to talk about lead generation. This might not be something that is particularly exciting to you, but it's vital to build a register of qualified contacts. These are people that are most likely to respond to, and purchase from, your company.

Who you send an email campaign to is more important than the content of the email.

Let me repeat that.

Who you send an email campaign to is more important than the content of the email.

If you send a poorly thought out pitch to a cleaned contact list of Fortune 500 CEOs, odds are you'll still get some kind of response. But the same second-rate pitch sent to an uncleaned list, with a high bounce rate, will send you straight to spam. And that's never somewhere that we want to be!

AVOIDING IRRELEVANT EMAILS

But before we go any further, let me answer an obvious question that you probably have. Why is this important?! Why can't you just send emails to anyone and everyone? Well, you can do this if you want, but if you send emails to people that are not interested, you will end up with significantly lower response rates, and the risk of heading straight to spam. This is something that you want to avoid at all costs. And if you're sending people irrelevant emails, even if you've appropriately warmed up your inbox and have the greatest cold email in the world, you can still be marked as spam. The more inappropriate contacts that you pester with irrelevant emails, the more likely it is that you will end up ruining your email account.

Cold email is not spam, so don't make it into spam.

So it is vital that you have watertight lead generation criteria. This will ensure that your whole operation remains above board, and that you're being helpful rather than a nuisance. Lead generation is not about firing out as many emails as possible, it's about identifying people who need your services, and, critically, who can afford to pay the price that you want.

In order to achieve this, we need to put lead generation criteria in place. The first part of this process is to address a few points that are required in order to send effective cold emails. These are first and last name, email, website, company name, and the custom first line. Those five data points are all that you really need for each lead.

All of this information can be found online, with the exception of the custom first line; you will obviously have to write that yourself! But in order to identify this information, we first need to define our target market. And there are three points that are required — we need to know a specific industry, job title and company size.

TARGETING THE INDUSTRY

Beginning with the industry, you should approach this based on your case study and get hyper-specific. In the previous chapter, we talked about the pre-work and niching down your case studies. So you can now use that case study in order to find out who will buy from you. And it's important to really drill down into the specifics of what you're trying to achieve. As mentioned previously, eCommerce is not adequate. Instead, it should be precise

— subscription boxes, apparel, tool manufacturers, or whatever suits your particular needs. You don't just target startups, you look for B2B, SaaS, consumer apps, machine learning — again, whatever meshes with your operation.

A lot of people make a rookie error early on, believing that they're selling to startups across the board, when B2B and B2C startups are completely different. Even within the specific niches, a B2C startup, in a pre-traction state, with $500 million raised in capital is nothing like a bootstrapped B2C that's in post-traction with thousands of established customers. They are completely different businesses, and yet both will often be described as startups. So it's extremely important that you distinguish between companies that you are targeting, and work out precisely which ones will suit your particular business.

You really can achieve anything with this technique; you can make the most obscure pitches to the most specific industries. For example, at one time we were doing lead generation for an event management startup. This whole industry is based on people that hold large events. But actually identifying these people is far from straightforward, as there was no database of event organizers at the time.

So our first step was to generate a lead pool. In order to achieve this, we began by assembling a list of the top events, and then segmented it down to just New York City (where this agency was based). We then worked our way backwards from that list to find the names of the organizers, and then their contact details. Only at this point were we able to email these people and start booking meetings.

The great thing about contacting people in niche industries is that no one else can identify them either! So they don't get bothered very much! In many ways, targeting niche and very specific industries is better, as they simply receive considerably less contact. You can even think outside the box and attend conferences and events; anything that enables you to come into contact with people that you're targeting.

But the important thing to remember is that there is no limit to what you can achieve with cold email. There are no boundaries or goals that you can't pursue. You might have to get creative, but this whole strategy can connect you with anyone or anything.

JOB TITLES

Once you've settled on the industry, the second point that you need to address is job title. I'm sure you'll agree that it's logical to aim as high as possible in this department. I almost always begin with the CEO, as it's best to go straight for the top immediately. Now you probably want to stop me right there. You might say that "You're intending to sell to a major enterprise, and it's obviously pointless to email the CEO of Morgan Stanley, as he's never going to reply." What I would say to that is that we actually received a response from the CEO of Morgan Stanley, and he booked a meeting with the Director of Marketing, who is maybe three levels below him in the company. Nothing is impossible. Yes, there are obviously times that you don't get the response that you're looking for, but then you can aim a bit lower. If you don't aim high to begin with, you never know whether or not you would have been successful.

If there's no response from the CEO, make your way down the corporate ladder of command step-by-step, one title at the time, every two weeks. Target the Chief Marketing Officer, then the Director of Marketing, then the Senior Brand Manager, then the Associate Brand Manager. It's also important not to email two people from the same company simultaneously. Only deal with one contact at a time, or you run the risk of spamming them. Or two people could see your email, show it to each other, and then see that it's a mass email, at which point your response rate drops and your risk of spam goes through the roof!

What I found is that, especially in offices, it's better to have the Director of Marketing tell the Director of Technology about you, and for them to enter into an organic conversation. The alternative is that the Director of Marketing discusses your message with the Director of Technology, and they come to the conclusion that you've been spamming both of them. It's better to email just one person, and to have them be the unique individual in the company who discovers your services and worth.

COMPANY SIZE

The third important attribute is the size of the company. As I've discussed previously, we usually target Golden

Geese companies that are worth between $5 million and $150 million in annual revenue. But I want to emphasize once more, smaller businesses and local commerce can be contacted, but they're harder to close big deals with. And you can sell to the big corporations; we've arranged meetings with Coca-Cola, Dunkin' Donuts, Morgan Stanley, and many other familiar names. But the process is longer and more arduous. That's why the golden geese companies are the best to work with. They have more money than a small business, but don't have such a vast management and organizational structure to contend with.

So your homework for this section is to identify the following for your target customer — industry, company size, and job title.

The next thing that you need is a list of email addresses that are ripe for cold emails. There are various ways you can achieve this, but one thing I recommend is checking out the list of all my favorite lead generation tools at **coldemailmanifesto.com/tools**. We keep this page up to date and ensure that our specific recommendations are always the top solutions on the market. That's why I'm reluctant to put any of this in the book, as the situation can change quite rapidly. But we keep on top of things, and post all of the most important and relevant information at **coldemailmanifesto.com/tools**, so that you don't have to do the hard work of researching and understanding this.

LEAD SCRAPING

Lead scraping is the first technique that you can use to generate leads, and this is a manual lead generation process. This essentially means that you find a list of companies online, and generate your email list from this research. For example, you might search for top airlines, or go to LinkedIn and seek out a specific criteria. Then you run a lead scraping tool that will pull data from that website, and generate it within a document. This is a very manual process, and it does benefit from using one of the tools that we recommend at the aforementioned web link. These tools enable you to verify those emails, which in turn reduces your bounce rate. It is all a crucial part of making the process as efficient as possible, as well as retaining the credibility of your email inbox.

And then you would send emails based on those manual leads that have been scraped via this process. This is not necessarily the best way to generate leads, but it is definitely the most affordable. Lead scraping tends to appeal to a lot of beginners, and I wouldn't necessarily condemn this if you're on a tight budget. However, I don't typically recommend this approach, as it's easier to hire people that intimately understand lead generation, as you will simply get much better results.

LEAD DATABASES

Another thing that I recommend for any business, even those with a particularly small budget, is utilizing the array of lead generation databases that already exist.

Again, all of the tools that are required for this particular process are listed at **coldemailmanifesto.com/tools**. I can't put my current recommendation into this book, as I want it to remain relevant and accurate indefinitely. And I don't want people using tools and believing them to be the best available, when the market has evolved and changed.

Regardless of this, if the tool that you select is any good, you'll be able to search by industry and revenue, plus a bunch of other criteria. There are even some leading tools that offer custom first line writing, and allow you to send from there, which can be a useful asset when you're first getting the hang of cold email.

ONLINE FREELANCERS

The third valuable source of leads is online freelancers. There are a huge number of job boards available online, and at the time of writing the most notable is Upwork. These platforms can be used to hire a freelancer to conduct your lead generation. Job boards are great because they are used by people all over the world. They are becoming increasingly credible, and this means that you can hire lead generators that have been trained by the top companies on the planet — Salesforce, Cisco Systems, Oracle, and many other businesses that are killing it with outreach.

This enables you to acquire a cheap, verified list of emails that are ready to go out of the box. What I will typically do to find freelancers is hire 3–4, and test the emails that they send using an email verification tool. This helps me figure out which ones are legitimate, and if we find that one or two of the people we've hired have done an excellent job, we'll keep them around on a more permanent basis.

There can be situations where the lead quality is really poor, but then you can receive a refund if the hire has failed to deliver. However, I very rarely do this, as I view the whole process as a test. But if what I receive is clearly a reused lead list, or a scam, then I will claim a refund. It's difficult to recommend pricing for this particular task, as it can vary greatly depending on the market and the people that you hire. What I can say is that there is a huge number of people available that can offer value in lead generation, and you can negotiate and bring them on board at a price point that makes sense for your company and the person you're hiring.

CONCLUSION

In summary, lead generation is an important part of the cold email process. It plays a critical role in ensuring that your operation is efficient, and also helps prevent your email inbox from becoming spammy. It can be done relatively inexpensively, and it's worthwhile to invest that money in order to get the results that you need. Generally speaking, cutting corners in life doesn't work, and it definitely doesn't work with cold email. You do need to invest some due diligence into the process if you want great results.

Your homework for this chapter is to generate a list of 100 leads using the methods we just discussed.

As with so many things in life, you will only get out of cold email what you put into it in the first place, so get to work!

TRAINING YOUR TEAM

You've seen everything that you need in order to get your team ramped up. You have the example email script. You know that you're measuring your team's performance, and that they are incentivized to deliver this. You even have the exact job postings in place that you're going to use to attract clients. You have everything that you need to succeed at this.

But if that's not enough, if you want informative videos and specific tactics that you can hand to your salespeople in order to train them up fully, head on over to **ColdEmailManifesto.com/courses**. We have built an entire series of training programs that outline exactly how to do this for your company. So you don't need to waste any time working out how to achieve this. If you want a done-for-you solution, please reach out to my agency X27 at x27marketing.com

That's the basic system in place. You're ready to go. So in the next chapter, we're going to look at writing your email scripts in detail.

Soon your operation will be running like clockwork!

CHAPTER 6.

The Perfect Cold Email

This is the most important chapter in this book. This is where I'm going to outline the anatomy of a perfect cold email. The five parts that go together to create a structure that will make you serious money.

I'm also going to show you some examples of emails that have worked for me and our clients. By the end of this chapter, you'll be ready to write your own perfect cold email that you can start testing immediately. This is going to be an action-oriented chapter, so I hope you're ready to do some work!

Here's the exact cold email we used to generate $600,000 in annual revenue in 30 days and then millions in revenue for our agency and clients:

Subject: Quick question
Hi Jackson,
Been following Fuzz for a while and love your work, awesome job with Rockefeller Center!

I specialize in finding new clients for web and app developers. Recently, we helped Dom and Tom, an NYC based developer, bring on McDonald's and close an extra $1,000,000 in 6 months.

Can you take on more clients at Fuzz? Let me know and I can send over a few times to chat.

Thanks,
Alex

—

Alex Berman | Founder
EXPERIMENT 27
12249 McKinnon Rd, Windermere, FL 34786
Mobile: 972 922 9823
alex@x27marketing.com | x27marketing.com

To reiterate, a great cold email consists of five parts:

- Subject line
- Compliment
- Case study
- Call to action
- Email signature

We're going to take a look at each of these in more detail, and I'm going to walk you through everything that you need to know.

BUYING FROM STRANGERS

But before we do that, I want you to ask yourself an important question. What would it take for you to buy something from a complete stranger? That's a very important question, as that's essentially what you're doing here. Contacting someone out of the blue with a proposition, and they know absolutely nothing about you whatsoever. So you have to be convincing. You have to grab their attention rapidly. Whenever you're writing a cold email you should keep this concept in mind, as it will ultimately define whether or not you're successful.

After you grab the attention of your potential client, the next thing you need to do is convey authority. This can be achieved by delivering great value upfront, cutting through all of the noise and doubts that will no doubt be reverberating around the mind of this customer. Your job with cold email is to eliminate these doubts, and make the client believe that they simply have to get in contact with you. Not all of these initial contacts will turn into sales, but if you can deliver the percentages that we've discussed elsewhere in the book, you are definitely going to generate a lot more business.

This part of the process is addressed by three parts of the cold email that I've mentioned above — The C's: compliment, case study, and call to action. The compliment gets their attention, the case study sets authority, and the call to action induces them to book a meeting. And this is all achieved in three sentences. That doesn't sound too labor-intensive, does it?

Okay, let's go through some examples. Here's a script for mobile development.

Subject line: Quick question, Jack

Hi Jack,

Huge fan of Acme Inc. and your forward thinking approach to marketing!

Recently I've helped several companies build VR applications in order to drive more awareness to their brands and I'd love to do the same for you.

Mind if I send over a few times for a quick call?

Thanks,

Alex

It's important to emphasize that this company is being extremely specific. Drill down into something that you know is relevant to the client. Don't just tell them that you do app development — everyone does app development, so what?!

Here's another example for a pay per click advertising campaign:

Subject line: Quick question

Hi Greg,

Hope your day is going well so far — just came across Acme so thought I'd reach out.

Recently helped Globonet, a technology company, use email, LinkedIn advertising, and content marketing to advertise their product, which resulted in 500+ leads and $2M in revenue within a year.

Would love to help you do something similar for Acme — mind if I send over a few times to chat?

Thanks,

Alex

ANOTHER EXAMPLE FOR BRAND STRATEGY:

Subject line: Call next week?

Hi Jackson,

Came across Acme recently and fell in love with <specific product>!

Recently finished the website and marketing materials for Globonet, where they saw a 97% annual increase in mobile traffic. Would love to do the same and help take the Acme brand to the next level.

Mind if I send over some available times for a call next week?

Best Regards,
Alex

It's a really simple process, but it's important to get each part of that process in place. So let's move on to writing the perfect cold email.

SUBJECT LINE

The logical place to start is with the subject line. But why is this even important? Quite simply, your subject line is your first point of contact with a potential prospect. It's the first thing that they see in the inbox, and they're going to judge you based on this. They're only going to see this and your name, so you need to make it good. This is the deciding factor as to whether your email will be opened or deleted.

We're going to give you a bunch of great examples in just a second. But, first, it's important to understand that a good subject line is direct. It's short and to the point. Often you're dealing with people who are extremely busy, and you need to make an instant impact with them. Plus, if your subject line is too long, the full thing won't even be visible in the email inbox.

Your subject line shouldn't be more than five words, and ideally two words. It needs to prick the curiosity of the recipient so that they absolutely have to click it. This is one area in which it's fine to be clickbait! You want them to think about what it could be, but not be able to know without opening the email.

And, finally, many good subject lines will be personalized. This isn't always the case, and, in fact, the number one subject line that we use breaks this rule immediately! But all of the other ones that we use are personalized, meaning that you include their name, possibly the company name… something that identifies it as being specific. Again, this separates your email from emails that will be perceived as spam and it demonstrates that it's actually directed at the recipient.

But to make this as easy as possible for you, I'm going to give you our 10 top subject lines right now that have proven to be successful:

- Quick Question
- [Name], Quick Question
- Quick Question, [Company Name]
- <Relevant emoji>
- Question?
- Something for you, [Name]

- Interview Invite
- I've got a Story for You
- [Name] Recommended I Get in Touch
- Intro

"Quick Question" is without a doubt the most effective subject line. But it's certainly worthwhile to test some of the other examples out, as you may experience different results in your particular field. I should mention that the emoji-based example was because we were pitching to game developers — you should use something relevant to another industry. The emoji changes based on the offer and recipient, but you can play around with that and see what works for you. For example, when we sold to breweries, a beer emoji worked well.

PERSONALIZED FIRST LINES

The second part of the process is to create an excellent personalized first line. Again, the aim here is to compel the recipient to respond. As mentioned previously, this is based around a custom compliment. This isn't always the easiest thing to write, and it can even feel a little cringy. But it's simply the most effective way of connecting with clients.

I'm sure that the prospect of writing personalized cold emails is not necessarily an attractive one. You probably want to skip this section. We all do. No one wants to put in the actual work of writing personalized cold emails; I barely want to do it! The only reason we use this approach is that it's 10 times more effective than not personalizing.

If we could get away without personalizing, we would definitely skip the whole process. And there are times where if you niche down enough you can write a first line that appeals to everyone in your niche, or create a first line that has one personalized data point that you can outsource: for instance, for cosmetics you could write:

Hi Jack, my girlfriend was just telling me about how much she loves {!Company name} especially the {!Product Name} and I figured it was worth reaching out directly.

If you can't find a system like that, then a custom compliment is something that will separate you from the potentially thousands of other messages that important people receive. It's going to identify you as the wheat that will be separated from the chaff. So it's definitely worth investing a few minutes in order to set the wheels in motion for deals that could be worth tens of thousands or even hundreds of thousands of dollars. It just makes sense!

An example of a custom compliment would be similar to the million-dollar email script that we talked about previously:

"I've been following Fuzz for a while, love your work. Awesome job with Rockefeller Center."

That's something very specific that shows you understand what the client has been doing.

That's one example. Here are several more.

- Hey Dennis, huge fan of what you're doing at x.ai — we use it all the time internally.

- Hey Dennis, came across your thoughts on Google Duplex, it's interesting — I love your approach to company disclosure.
- Hey Dennis, been following your career since Visual Revenue, and I'm hugely impressed with what you've built at x.ai
- Hey Dennis, been following your story for a while and finally checked your LinkedIn, impressed that you have a patent.
- Hey Dennis, love that quote on your LinkedIn about Bjorn — it's amazing how you've incorporated that irreverence into your entire brand.
- Hey Marcy, greetings from a fellow UC grad!
- Hey Marcy, been following WPromote for a while now and impressed with your background…amazing that you went from sales associate to director of marketing!
- Hey Marcy, love what you're doing at WPromote, especially the work you did with Pied Piper :-P
- Hey Marcy, huge fan of Zenni, so when I saw that you ran their campaigns I had to reach out!
- Hey Marcy, love the work you did with Weiner-schnitzel.
- Hey Hayley, love everything about Golden Hippo, and am impressed with your background in IT.
- Hey Hayley, found you on LinkedIn and love what you're doing — amazing that you point out how critical listening is, I believe the same thing.

- Hey Hayley, came across Golden Hippo and love that quote from Alyssa on your website, it's impressive that you treat the QA team so well.
- Hey Hayley, saw you were hiring a business analyst, and wanted to reach out and say congrats on the growth!
- Hey Hayley, been following the Golden Hippo Instagram for a while, and love how you treat the IT team.

Okay, so now you get the general idea. That was way too many compliments, but now you have an example of nearly every type of compliment you can write. You can complement the recipient on company news, department news, their career, revenue, stock price, anything specific, as long as it has been reported on recently. Just don't go too far. A well-written first line will have just enough information to indicate that you've personalized it, but not so much that you appear to be a stalker! Keep that in mind — the shorter, the better. One sentence is enough.

I also want to mention something really important at this point. There are loads of AI tools out there that claim to write custom first lines. They're getting better all the time and I see a future where they replace humans soon, but as of this publish date they are not ready.

Right now, the best thing to do is write them yourself. Once you've done 100, you can hire a custom first line writer on Upwork. But I always recommend doing the work first before you hire someone to do it. So your homework for this section is to write 100 custom first lines; one for each of the leads that you generated in the last chapter.

HOMEWORK

Write 100 custom first lines, one for each lead from the previous chapter.

CASE STUDY

The next part of the process is the case study. And a perfect example would be going back to the million-dollar email that we used at X27, which helped to generate $600,000 in annual recurring revenue in just 60 days and millions after that. Here is the case study included in that email:

> I specialize in finding new clients for web and app developers. Recently, we helped Dom & Tom — an NYC-based developer, bring on McDonald's and close an extra $1 million in six months.

Here are some hypothetical examples:

> Recently, we helped Marvel Studios get 250,000 Twitter followers in two weeks using targeted Twitter ads.

And another:

> Recently, we helped Palantir close $500,000 in new contracts in six months by using our brand guidelines and logo to increase their value.

And yet another:

Recently, we helped LinkedIn save $7 million on DevOps hires in 60 days by using our AI-powered recommendations.

So we need to write something like that for your company. Here's what to keep in mind:

A case study is not just about flaunting numbers. Every word of the case study is engineered. And every word of the case study is important. It's about demonstrating experience, instantly building authority, and curating the appropriate reaction from the recipient.

Interestingly, the common assertion that people need to know you and like you in order to purchase from you is actually nonsense! It's completely false. People don't need to like you; they simply need to trust you and know that you're going to deliver. An example of this would be Microsoft, a largely reviled company, yet they sell Windows all over the world, a largely reviled product! In obscene quantities! No one likes Bill Gates, and that doesn't make any difference whatsoever (sorry Bill!).

So here's your homework for this section. Look at the examples that we've provided, and translate three of your case studies into one-sentence case studies that could be used in a cold email. And if you feel that you need any assistance with this, we're more than willing to help you. Check out coldemailmanifesto.com/courses, and we'll handhold you through the whole process. If you're running into obstacles, don't put this book in the trash, please reach out.

HOMEWORK:

Translate three of your case studies into One Sentence Case Studies

CALL TO ACTION

The next stepping stone in the process is the call to action. This is the easiest element because it's pretty much the same every time.

Before we go any further, remember that the goal of your cold email is to arrange a meeting. That's why every email ends with a "yes" or "no" question. "Mind if I send over a few times for a quick call?", for example. It must be easy to accept or decline, as the people that you're prospecting are busy. They haven't got time to muck around! The goal of what you're doing is not to get them to click on your portfolio, or watch some sort of quirky, personalized video, or even to sign up to your email list. It's just to get them on a meeting so that you can close on a five to six-figure deal. Every other use of cold email is a waste of this powerful tool.

Another important aspect of the call to action is that it must be significant. You want to arrange a meeting, so don't waste your time discussing or asking for things that are unimportant. Don't ask for newsletter signups or some other such trivial nonsense! Ask for meetings that will lead directly to sales. Because your time is valuable, the recipient's time is valuable, and you don't want to waste it on things of no consequence. Equally, as we mentioned previously, you need to go in there with big box items. It's pointless selling a product worth $200 via cold email. If you have any doubts about what you're offering, add a zero to the price, and you can thank me later!

The first example of a call to action that works is the 'simple ask'. "Interested? Let me know and I can send over a few times to chat." And the other we refer to as the 'specific benefit'. This one is a little more advanced. "Can you take on more clients? Let me know. And I can send over a few times to chat." The reason that the second one is more advanced is because of the first few words, which are customized to your exact offer, rather than copy pasting the same sentence as everyone else.

So your homework for this section is particularly straightforward! Just add the simple ask example to your email script. It can be copy and pasted without difficulty, and will still work perfectly well for your business.

HOMEWORK:

Add the Simple Ask to your cold email script.

I also wanted to mention briefly at this point that it's important to follow up on your initial email without spamming. We've already discussed this in the "Run Outbound Emails" section of Chapter 3, and it is important for you to follow those templates closely. One thing I should also reiterate is that if you are attempting to sell a big product to a client via cold email, and they indicate some interest, it's absolutely fine to continue emailing them. You should chase them down if they have expressed any intention of purchasing a $50,000 product, and if you fail to do so then you're a terrible salesperson!

Usually after initial positive feedback, I will follow up until I get a "yes" or "no", even if it takes months or years.

DEALING WITH THE PROCESS

Now I realize that this chapter has been particularly detailed, and that there are some very specific examples included. I also know that sometimes the process involved is not particularly inspiring or appetizing. And I'm also aware that you might not want to do this. You might think that it sounds like a laborious process, and you simply can't be bothered.

That's fine. You don't have to do anything in this life that you don't want to do. No one is forcing you to do this. But I do wish to reiterate the value of this process. I used to get paid $800 an hour to walk people through how to write the perfect cold email script. People wanted to pay me more, but I don't do one on ones as I just don't like consulting for businesses I don't own. That's because this is extremely valuable information, which is worth billions of dollars to companies all over the world collectively.

We put all of this information in this book for you, which you have purchased for only a couple bucks. I hope I'm not guilty of blowing my own trumpet, but you are receiving something extremely valuable for a meager amount of money. What you choose to do with this valuable information is entirely up to you. You don't have to do anything with it whatsoever. But if you don't implement the lessons that we've provided here, you're missing out on an absolutely huge opportunity. And I believe that no business, no matter how successful, can afford to miss out on this.

If you still have questions, please feel free to ask us by joining the private community or booking a consulting call with somebody on our team. You can do that at **coldemailmanifesto.com/courses**. This includes a private community and the opportunity to contact my cofounder Robert Indries and myself directly. We will provide further assistance in writing your cold email script or taking your campaigns to the next level.

Do not let any roadblock stop you from mastering cold email. Don't allow the nagging voice in your head, the one that always encourages you to be lazy to win! Please invest the effort required to master cold email. Because it is the most effective way to book meetings, particularly in the five to six-figure range for your business.

And wouldn't it be great to have a calendar full of those meetings arranged for next week?

CHAPTER 7.

Hit Send

By now you've unlocked the secret of cold email. You know how it works and you know how it's going to change your business. You're just about ready to hit 'Send'. But before you do that, there are quite a few questions that need to be answered.

HOW MANY EMAILS?

First things first… how many emails are you going to send? Are you going to be shooting off thousands every day? Or are you looking at a solitary email per day? That's the first question that we're going to address in this section.

When you approach cold email for the first time, the principle that I want you to keep in your head is slow and steady wins the race. The hare and the tortoise. You're not going to grow rapidly, you're going to build up gently, gaining momentum over time.

It's natural to want to jump in at the deep end. But if you begin too forcefully with cold email campaigns, you could hit a couple of issues immediately. First, your campaign isn't appropriately optimized. You might send 1,000 emails and find that your open rate is only 17%. This would naturally indicate that something is broken in the system. You might think: "fine, we'll fix it", but it's not as simple as that. You've now burned leads, put yourself at risk of getting marked as spam, and (worst of all) sent a campaign that could have performed 8x better with a few tweaks.

However, if you're more patient then you can eventually reach the point where you're sending 1,000 emails a day or more, obtaining a much higher open rate, booking way more meetings and closing a lot more deals as a result. If you start small, there's no reason that you can't improve your open rate to 80%, and get your meeting book rate to 6% or higher.

It's also worth bearing in mind that when it comes to scaling up, by the time you're in a position to send 1,000 emails it might not be something that you even wish to do. If you book 6 meetings for every 100 emails, 1,000 emails a day will lead to 60 meetings per day, which for most small businesses will require a ton of new hires. That's why you want to get to the point where your cold email campaigns are so effective and predictable that you can choose the number you send out in order to get the exact result you need. So you know that you can be successful with a relatively small number of emails. Less work with better results makes sense, right?

But if you want to get to that point, you have to optimize things correctly. The first thing I would recommend is to relisten the section on email warmup. This is not an optional extra, it's essential. You must warm up your email inbox for at least two weeks before sending, otherwise you will be marked as spam, and you'll have to start all over again.

Now, let's move onto scaling emails. During the first week, you should send 10 cold emails per day. You can then increase that by 10 emails every day for the first month, until you're averaging 100 customized emails per day. All the time that you're doing this, you should be keeping track of the total number of emails that you've sent, including follow-ups. This will enable you to avoid hitting any maximum email limits imposed by Gmail or Outlook.

Just keep things steady for a while, so that you can test the process diligently and hold on to your domain. After the first month is over, you can check your spam score using online tools, and if there are any red flags or noticeably increased spam rates, you can slow the process down. Or if everything is functioning according to plan, you can then begin to increase the numbers.

One thing that many people don't know is that Gmail has a maximum number of emails that you can send on a daily basis. If you sign up for the trial account, you can send out 2,000 emails every day at the time of writing. Bear in mind that if you're sending 1,000 cold emails every day, and then following up on quite a few of them, it's easy to get close to that 2,000 figure pretty quickly. So before you get anywhere near this number, make sure that your campaigns are functioning correctly.

Another important principle is to ensure that every single email that you send is being directed towards an email address that could eventually result in a purchase. This isn't a spray and pray approach! We're following a targeted and customized cold email strategy. Research each prospect on your lead list before you send your email. Look at their website and check whether they're a good fit for your service, and if it's the right size of company to target. This is also a great time to write your custom first line. Do your research, stick to your sending limits, and you can begin to build momentum.

Don't scale your campaign unless you're hitting the benchmarks. If you're not hitting your targets, your approach can improve, so get things right on a small scale before you begin to expand your operation. Otherwise you're wasting leads (and money).

BEST TIME TO SEND

Another question that coaching clients ask is the best time to send emails. The first thing to think about when you address this is the way that people conduct their working lives. People tend to check their work emails at certain times of the day and week. So first thing in the morning and at the end of the working day are the best times to send emails, because these are the most likely times that people will check their email inboxes.

It's also important to take time zones into consideration. Make sure that you know where the person that you're sending an email is located, and also that you optimize your approach based on that location. And don't just take countries into consideration; the United States is split up into numerous time zones, so bear this in mind as well. 10am in Philadelphia is not 10am in San Francisco!

Different times of day also tend to work better for various job titles and positions. For example, CEOs tend to check their emails first thing in the morning and late at night, especially if they're in hyper-growth startups. It's also best to aim for Tuesday or Wednesday as your sending day, as just before the weekend, or first thing on Monday morning, doesn't really work. People don't care about emails ahead of the weekend! And they have too much to do on Monday morning. Another possibility is to send on Sunday afternoon, as we've found that a lot of people will be planning their week ahead of time, so this can be an excellent opportunity to catch busy people in particular.

SENDING YOUR FIRST CAMPAIGN

Okay, let's get ready to send your first campaign. You've done your exercises, you've completed the homework, you have your cold email written, and you understand what you're selling and who's going to buy it. So let's send some emails!

Before you get started, you should definitely head over to **coldemailmanifesto.com/tools**, where we will keep you updated on all of the latest software. This market can change, and in fact does change rapidly, but we keep on top of it so that you don't have to bother. Check out the tools recommendation page, and make sure that you use the latest and greatest software. I'd rather send you to an updated website than risk publishing a book with outdated information.

And I want to emphasize that things can go incredibly well with cold email, you can achieve things that are unimaginable. And, equally, it can go horrendously wrong, and you can have campaigns that go nowhere! But the important thing is that the whole process is a learning curve. As long as you're learning then you're one step closer to achieving success.

Let me give you an example of a campaign that went badly. Some years ago I wanted to start a company that was based on a database of SaaS tools. This would enable people to rank them and identify the perfect tool recommendation for their needs. So I made a list of companies that might require SaaS services. And the email itself was something like this:

Hey,

I'm doing research into starting a new SaaS company, and we'd love to know what issues you run into with SaaS tools.

What's the big problem with this email? It doesn't book a meeting and it doesn't target sales. So all we got back were some halfhearted answers. But this was THE recommended cold email strategy at the time!

If I was writing the email today, I might try the following:

Hey John,

I built a tool that gives you the ultimate SaaS recommendations for your company.

It starts at $5 a month, and you can get 10 recommendations to reboot all of the tools you're using, so that you can save more money and get more done.

Interested?

And from there you can actually judge whether someone is going to buy. That's the difference between when we tried and failed and what we do now. But it's all a learning curve. You're not going to nail everything the first time, second time, or even on your fiftieth attempt! But if you keep plugging away, keep learning, keep improving then there is so much that you can achieve with cold email.

So get those tools set up, queue your first campaign and hit send!

APPOINTMENT SETTING

Now it's not just enough to send an excellent cold email. You also need to go back and forth with the clients in order to book a meeting, in a process referred to as 'appointment setting'. So how do you do this? First, the most important principle to remember is that we're doing this to arrange a meeting. We're not selling via email; we want to get a phone call so that we can speak to the client directly. Therefore, every response to your cold email should be pushing towards this phone call, during which you're going to close the deal.

So let me give you a few scripts that we've used to book these meetings.

> Hey Mike,
> Sure thing. I'm free next week on Thursday and Friday between 12–1pm PST. Would either of those work for you?
> Thanks,
> Alex

And then you can continue to follow up if you don't hear from them again. There are various ways to deal with this, but one of my favorite responses is just:

> Bumping this up!

While on the subject, the initial meeting that you have with clients should only be 15–30 minutes. You're just testing the water, figuring out if they will be a good fit for you, and, more importantly, whether or not they can afford your services.

Here's another example:

Hi Jeff,
Would Tuesday at 1:30pm or 2pm PST work?
Let me know, and I can send over a calendar invite.

Thanks,
Alex

It's important to always give specific times for meetings, because it's easier for the client to book, and avoids a needless back and forth conversation. One thing I have found is that busy people appreciate it if you take the initiative, so don't feel that you need to pussyfoot around. Another tip here is that although there are calendar booking tools available, you might find that many high-level executives are over 50, and have a hard time with modern technology. My experience is that offering time slots is better than providing calendar invites.

Here's another example:

Hey Meredith,
How about next week?

Any day between 11:30am and 12:30pm or 5:30pm and 6:30pm PST would be best on my end.

Let me know if any of those times work for you.

Regards,
Alex

Another important issue is the best time to book the meetings. You will have the most luck booking meetings during the working days of your clients. If you're on UK time and your clients are in the US, be prepared to send meetings during your early morning and late evening.

So that's how to go about booking the meeting. But not everything will always go according to plan. We have to expect the unexpected! What happens if someone doesn't show up? Let's go through the process of trying to avoid this as much as possible.

NO SHOWS

You can't make everyone turn up, but you can definitely minimize the number of no shows.

First, you need to send a clear invite, and ensure that all of the details involved are correct. Make sure that it's crystal clear where the meeting is taking place and also that the person you're meeting with knows exactly what they need to do in order to join. And you should follow up on this by sending an email before the meeting that reminds them of the time and place, and provide a video chat link.

Then the next part of the process is to send an email five minutes before the meeting, reminding the recipient that they're speaking with you. My email for this simply says the following:

Mark,
Talk to you in five minutes! Here's the link: <>

Thanks,
Alex

By doing this, you are ensuring that everyone you contact sees your invitation three separate times.

But that still might not be enough! They still might not show up! So if you're sitting around for five minutes, you can send them another email informing them politely that you're "on the line when [they're] ready". If that doesn't work, you can call them directly. If the call isn't answered, leave a voicemail:

"Hey, it's Alex Berman calling at the scheduled time. Will give you a call back in 5 minutes or give me a call at 972-212-3818. Thanks!"

And then if nothing happens after a further five minutes, call back again and leave another voicemail:

"Hey, It's Alex calling. We were supposed to talk five minutes ago. I'll send you an email to reschedule. Thanks."

If a client fails to meet on three separate occasions, then send a breakup email, similar to some of the emails that we've discussed earlier in the book. One final opportunity to make contact.

Hey Mike,
I guess now is not a good time to discuss building a new website for you.

If you're still interested, you can get in touch with me here, or via the number in my signature.

Thanks,
Alex

Personally, I don't like to invest too much time in people that don't show up. But you might be more patient than me! Or you might be early on in the process and feel that the investment effort is worth it. I definitely wouldn't wish to label this as a mistake, but I would suggest that you shouldn't follow up any more than three times with anyone. If someone is really keen to make contact with you, they'll make it easy for you. You know, if you keep asking a woman out over and and over again, and she keeps making excuses, she probably doesn't want to go out with you!

If you want even more examples of these scenarios included, head over to our course "The Inbox", which features over 60 cold email conversations that lead to a booked meeting that you can tap into and customize for your own needs. You can join this course at **coldemail-manifesto.com/inbox**.

BENCHMARKS AND IMPROVING YOUR CAMPAIGN

Okay, I don't want to go over benchmarks too much, as we've discussed them elsewhere in the book, but it's important to reiterate what you should be aiming for. Your open rate should be 80%, your response rate should be at least 15%, and your meeting booking rate should be between 4% and 8%. The subject line and the quality of your leads will be the most important factors in achieving these benchmarks, so that's the first place to look if you don't hit your targets.

But how else can you improve your campaign in order to boost your figures? The first thing to note is that you can't expect major success immediately. Anything worth doing takes time, and this principle definitely applies to cold email. As I just explained, you need to build slowly and scale over time. You're definitely not going to get everything perfect immediately. If you think this is going to be an instant silver bullet, where you send 50 emails and your calendar is booked solid, you're going to be tremendously disappointed. That's just not realistic. You will only get out of this what you invest in it, and the process of cold email requires three Ts in addition to the the 3 C's — time, training and tenacity.

If you're not willing to put in the initial hard work, you won't get the results that you're looking for, and that would suck. So I want to emphasize that you do need to be patient, be fully invested in the process, and be willing to tweak and re-tweak everything involved in your cold email operation. But if you come to the table with the right attitude, you can achieve an enormous amount with the system outlined in this book. It might take six months, but you will get there if you are fully committed to the process.

That being said, one of the most important ways to improve cold email results is via lead quality. Ensuring that you only send emails to people who are likely to purchase from you. Prospects will only respond when they understand what you're selling, so if your response rate is disappointing that means either that your email is failing to get your point across succinctly, recipients judge it to be spam, or, worse still, that your offer is completely irrelevant to your target market. So focus on making your one-sentence case study as clear as possible. Make your emails short and to the point, and ensure that they are absolutely crystal clear.

If you find that you're running into issues, show the email that you're sending to a friend. Have them read it and then tell you what you sell. If they can't do this, it means that your email needs to be rewritten, and made more straightforward and direct. This issue can cause a lot of difficulties, particularly in the technology field where the disparity and use cases between various companies can be hard to talk about in a simple manner. So definitely focus on this if you're selling a tech product or service.

Response rate is the key benchmark. If you're getting responses, then you're well on the way to success. However, if you have a strong response rate, but you're not managing to book meetings, you need to review your follow-up strategy and appointment setting approach. Remember that you should be aiming for 6+ meetings per 100 emails sent.

The easiest way to book more meetings is to reduce the amount of time between their response and your follow-up. So if someone indicates interest, get back to them within 5 minutes and watch your meeting book rate soar!

If you're dealing with busy and important people, they don't want to mess around. You have to convince them that you're extremely valuable to them, and you need to do this rapidly. Otherwise they'll forget about you, get rid of you, and move on to something else, without ever giving you a second thought.

Another key issue is bounce rate. You must ensure that this is kept under 8% at all times. Make sure that you verify your emails before sending, and constantly review the quality of your email leads. If you have inconsistent issues with your bounce rate, it's time to find a new lead database. There's nothing worse than putting effort in and knowing that it's been completely wasted, so you really need to keep on top of this issue.

TESTING PLAN

It's also important to test your cold email strategy on a regular basis. Keep trying different things to see how they affect the overall process and your results. Here are a few suggestions.

- For every 100 emails that you send, try 50% with one subject line and 50% with another.
- Try different case studies and experiment with the wording.
- Change the sending times for different days and hours.
- Swap follow-up emails, try different wording and approaches.

For each of these strategies, remove anything that turns out to be ineffective, and even do more testing with different proportions and combinations. The choice is yours, but what you shouldn't do is proceed to cold email without measuring the process and regularly attempting different approaches.

INCREASING COLD EMAIL RESULTS

Here are more things you can do to increase your results. Now everything is in place for you to execute your cold email strategy. But I would like to talk about some advanced tactics that you can use to take your cold email campaigns to the next level. There are other softer things that you can implement in order to increase your results above a normal level of optimization.

The biggest thing that you can do to compel prospects to respond is to build trust. You want your clients to feel that you're an expert, trust that you are a responsible person to work with, and believe that their investment of time and money is secure and wise. So if you want to increase your cold email results astronomically, you need to increase the amount of trust that the client has in you proportionately.

But how do you build trust?! The first way is to deliver a strong and extremely relevant case study that speaks directly to the recipients. The stronger that case study is, and the more relevant that they are to the specific industry that you're targeting, and the more that they speak to the particular person that you're contacting, the greater the amount of trust that you are going to build. The ideal scenario would be a case study involving work with a competitor, because then you have social proof of something in common with the target. That equals instant trust building, and that's money in the bank.

The second way is the no-brainer offer. If you really want a client to trust you, your no-brainer offer needs to be something that requires no thought whatsoever. So if you want to strike gold with a cold email, you need to make sure that your offer appeals to your target market. So that someone reads it and instantly wants to buy from you.

And the third and final way that you can increase your cold email success is to establish a personal brand that illustrates that you're an expert in your field. This can be done via social media accounts, or YouTube, podcasts, blogs, or an active website presence. It's just anything that will demonstrate to people that you have authority in your field. Having links online that back up the assertions that you make in your cold email will exponentially increase your results. For a good example, check out what we've built with the Alex Berman and Robert Indries personal brands.

If you would like assistance with all of that stuff, I recommend joining one of our courses. Because they go through exactly how to set up your agency website, how to get your case study in line, and how to sell yourself in a way that establishes your personal brand. This book is focused on cold email, but if you want all of the other stuff, you should definitely head over to **ColdEmailManifesto.com/courses** and see what we have to offer.

So if you follow everything that we've done so far consistently, you will have not only the perfect cold email, but a campaign that prints money. That's the ultimate goal. It won't happen immediately, so if you don't succeed at first, keep trying, keep testing, keep refining. Because if you stick with this, you will find success eventually.

And that's all I want you to keep telling yourself. Everyone that has gotten this to work is shocked! They feel like they unlocked a superpower! They can make money from anyone and anything at any time. So make sure that you push through the hard times. Clients will tell you that they're not interested, people will tell you to quit cold email, even your friends and family will tell you that it sucks!

But if you push through, you get through to the other side, and you're going to experience massive success. It just depends how much you want it.

CHAPTER 8.

Building A Team of Rockstars

W e've talked a lot in this book about the process of setting up cold email. About all of the prep work that you need to do, and all of the specifics involved in getting started and being successful.

But that's not the whole picture. There are also some softer skills involved. We need to talk about mindset, about happiness, and about how you set the business up so that your employees relish the process, and you grow and succeed as a result.

JOB SATISFACTION

The first thing to consider is that job satisfaction is important. When you're a business owner, this can sometimes fly under the radar. Businesspeople tend to assume that everyone is as excited about the process as they are. But that's not necessarily the case. The onus is on you, as the person who is setting up and managing your business, to ensure that everyone is pulling in the same direction.

Because not everyone is happy. I am extremely fortunate. I'm living my dream life. I'm booking clients whenever I want, I've got a seven-figure agency, I'm literally writing a book right now; my life is like a dream come true. But most people are not living their dream lives. The majority of people wake up at a time that they don't want to wake up, sit in meetings that are tedious and annoying, and are selling something that they don't truly believe in. In short, they don't enjoy their everyday lives.

Now you don't need to be an expert on psychology to guess whether people that enjoy their work or people that don't enjoy their work will be more productive and successful. How can you ever truly engage with something that you don't believe in, or even hate doing? You might be able to give 100% commitment for a certain period of time, but it's only human nature that this will slide rapidly, as you become increasingly bored by the process. And once you decide that something is tedious, it becomes a massive chore, you check out mentally, and this is when your results inevitably deteriorate.

So if you can move your employees from a position of finding work to be an endless grind, to enjoying the work that they're doing, you win. They're going to buy into the process, they're going to achieve more, and you're going to make more profit as a result. Leaving aside the bottom line, it's just more enjoyable to manage people who believe in what they're doing. If everyone is on the same page, it just makes your working life so much more rewarding.

But here is the million-dollar question… how do you actually ensure that your employees are happy at work? Well, I'm writing a book about cold email here; it's a powerful tool. And you'll find that when you've got a hammer, suddenly every problem becomes a nail!

Let me give you an example. When I was working at the New York agency, one of the first things that I did was meet with all of the director-level personnel at the company. This included the Director of Web for the agency, who I must say was a gruff developer-type! He worked with a bunch of major corporations, and was digging deep into some extremely technical and rather nerdy back-end operations. He was an expert in his field, but not someone who radiated positive energy!

Anyway, I arranged a 30-minute meeting with him, and asked him what he actually wanted to build. And he immediately began speaking so passionately, in a way that I hadn't witnessed before, about developing websites for music festivals. This got the cogs of my brain turning immediately.

As a result of this conversation, we were able to spin up a cold email campaign, pitch music festivals, and book meetings with several major ones. Not only was this profitable for the agency, but this previously serious and glum individual was now engaged, because he was involved with something that he was passionate about.

So if you're doing cold email effectively, and leveraging the superpower of being able to book meetings with anyone, you can use this technique to increase the morale of employees. This guy who I engaged with didn't have a problem working with major corporations, but it felt like a grind. Just by giving him this cherry on the cake, a fun project that he really believed in, it made the whole job much more enjoyable for him. And that means better engagement, better outcomes, better results, and more money!

This can be applied across the board for your business. Everyone has their own interests, everyone has their own internal artist, everyone has something that they're really passionate about. Identify what that is, and then build a business case that enables them to work on it. It might not be 100% of their projects. It might not be 10% of their projects. But if you can throw in some fun projects on a regular basis, maybe once a month, maybe every two months, you'll boost the happiness of your employees. And this is something that should never be neglected.

RECRUITING SALESPEOPLE

Recruitment is key in any business. And in the type of business we are discussing here, there is no one more important than the salespeople. But it's difficult to assemble a great sales team.

The first problem that you'll encounter is that the best salespeople in the world are freelancing, making millions of dollars every year. And the second-best salespeople are working for companies that compensate them extremely well; some of the biggest corporations on the planet. Your chances of matching their conditions are extremely small, and even if you could then they're not necessarily going to jump ship from where they are.

So that leaves you with the C-tier salespeople. That's just the reality of this business. If you're in a position to hire the best salespeople in the world, you don't really need to read this book, because you're already generating a massive amount of revenue!

The way to address this problem is to train people from the bottom up. Everyone needs a break when they start out, and there are extremely talented people out there who have yet to establish themselves as successful. You will have to accept that there will be significant churn in your sales team while you find your dream team, so this is something that you should keep in mind at all times.

But where do you recruit the best people? Well, I've had excellent experiences recruiting from the audiences of influencers. If I need to hire a salesperson, I will ask an existing influencer whether they're in contact with anyone that they consider to be up and coming. If you haven't personally established an audience, I highly recommend leveraging some people that do have audiences to get recommendations. Ask famous or mid-tier sales trainers and entrepreneurs. I have found that the best salespeople are young and super hungry — excited to the point of seeming coked-out! You want these Adderall-infused, chomping-at-the-bit, driven people to take your company to the next level.

Generally, you're going to find these people in Make Money Online spaces, particularly in the realm of affiliate marketing. That's where we found our best sales people, only now we have over a dozen commission-only salespeople who are eating what they kill. And these are all salespeople that closely follow the top gurus, that follow the top salespeople in the industry, and they're plugged into the top advice and tactics. Don't be afraid to lean into that area of the Internet in order to find your dream sales team.

ACHIEVING BUY-IN

Let me tell you the story of two salespeople that I worked with previously. Again, this is back at the agency in New York. I remember that this guy started, and he was the most hyped to achieve success of any salesperson I've ever seen. He was a late-career guy at the time, about 49 years-old, and he'd just been hired as a senior-level salesperson in the organization. He immediately brought recommendations to the table. He recruited a top NBA player to work with our agency, and connected us with several valuable clients, who were already friends of his.

But about two months into this guy's tenure at the company, he suddenly stopped recommending his friends. And his close rate plummeted. It tumbled from almost 100% to virtually nothing. In fact, one of the ways that I was able to become the top salesperson was simply picking up his slack and doing his proposals, because he had checked out completely.

So I asked him what was going on, why had there been this monumental change in his attitude? The answer? He had lost faith in the ability of our agency to deliver the work. For the first two months of his employment, he was hyped because he believed that we could do everything we promised, we were building valuable apps, and everything that we were doing was great. But something snapped. He lost his belief, the hype disappeared, and he no longer had any faith that we were going to deliver, at which point his sales immediately dissolved into nothing.

The lesson to learn from this is that the best salespeople believe in the service that they're delivering, they believe in the product. And so it's incumbent upon the manager and directors of the company to ensure that it is always delivering on its promises. That's the first part of the process. The equally important second part is to communicate this to your salespeople. Because if your people believe that you are changing the lives of your employees and clients, they will promote your company aggressively, get their friends on board, and they'll recruit anyone and everyone that they can possibly find to buy from your organization.

If they don't believe it, the exact opposite will happen. You might get a few exceptions. Some people are hugely professional, and they will achieve results selling something that they hate. But you definitely should not rely on this. Don't make it an option. You need to be delivering at the highest levels, and that means achieving buy-in across your organization. If you fix your production and delivery, and communicate this effectively to your salespeople, you'll find that even your worst-performing salesperson will become a top performer.

WHY YOU NEED AN AFFILIATE ARMY

You've probably noticed already that I advocate using commission-only salespeople. I'm also the first person to acknowledge that there is a huge debate on this subject. I'm also happy to concede that most companies do not use commission-only salespeople. I'll even tell you the arguments against it! People think that you shouldn't hire commission-only salespeople because if your product is hard to sell, they will give up. That's the primary reason. It could also be argued that if you have people on a commission-only basis, there is a rogue element to your workforce; there is always the possibility that they will simply disappear and do their own thing. Another possible argument against commission-only is that it can be harder to create a tight corporate culture than with salaried employees.

Those are all fair arguments, but I'll tell you what our organization does. Our team is 12 commission-only salespeople, although we're constantly expanding our operation. And we have experienced huge success with our team, who are generating leads, booking meetings, handling the cold outreach process, and closing deals.

So why does this work for us? We offer lead generation, which is a very easy thing to sell because we're changing people's lives. If you do lead generation, people want to buy it, particularly if you deliver on your promises. So we instantly leapt over that hurdle of needing salaried employees. If you lead a commission-only sales team, I call ours an Affiliate Army, you will see incredible results that would otherwise be impossible.

And there's a simple reason for this. Would I have been able to afford a dozen salespeople if I was paying each one $100,000 annual salary, or even $50,000? No, we definitely had to scale up to reach that level. But if you have your staff working on commission-only, paying just based on what they close, your whole operation grows organically. Your salespeople can potentially earn more than $100,000 annually, but this will only occur when they are successful. It's much more likely to create a win-win scenario.

Another important aspect of this is that you're going to experience most of your results from just 10% of your sales team. That's the way it works; the cream always rises to the top. So it is your job as a commission-only recruiter, as a manager and director of your sales operation, to move people out of your organization that aren't effective. Most people who are any good should be able to close deals within a couple of weeks. If they can't achieve this, get them out of there, as they will have no ultimate benefit to your organization. Effectively, they're wasting your money. With sales, you have to be aggressive. It's a wild world, and you can't afford to stand still. If you do, you won't succeed.

Firing people is never pleasant. You'd have to be pretty sociopathic to enjoy making someone redundant! And, of course, I don't. You know, I'm not gonna sit here and say I enjoy firing people. But there is a joy to it, like popping a festering pimple. Another obvious barrier that people experience is that they wonder whether the replacement staff will actually be better. But every meeting that is taken by a bad salesperson costs what that client would have potentially paid you. If a salesperson bungles a $100,000 deal...congratulations, you just lost $100,000! That's always the way I think about it. When you think about it in those terms, it makes it far more palatable to fire people that underperform. That last bad hire didn't cost you nothing — you paid him $0 in commission because he cost you millions.

In closing, I just want to emphasize that if you're opting for a commission-only model, you need to be aggressive about getting great people into your organization, and getting underperforming people out of your organization. If you can't do that, go for a salary model, but understand that you won't be able to scale as quickly. And if you can't fire people, you will fail in the long run.

SALES TRAINING

Finally, on the subject of sales, I would like to talk about sales training. Central to this is an important concept — there are essentially two types of managers.

One is the supportive father that will take their kids to the pool, and slowly but surely teach them how to swim. And there's the type that will throw their child straight in the deep end, and if they drown just get another kid!

Now, of course, I'm being slightly sarcastic! But I am the second type of person. My co-founder, Robert Indries, is the first type of manager. And there is absolutely room for both. Personally, I would much rather churn through employees in order to find the right salespeople. I possibly inherited this from my parents, as this was very much in their attitude when they were selling latex gloves. We had a very high churn rate, but we also had a superb sales team in terms of performance.

The best type of sales training is when you get your salespeople the information, you give them the tools that they need to do well, you set achievable goals together, and then you throw them into the pool to sink or swim. If they're not naturally talented, you get rid of them, and find someone better. I should emphasize that my cofounder Robert would say the complete opposite. He would say that you engage in a feedback loop with your salespeople, and then nurture the relationship as if they are clients. Both approaches can definitely work, but as this book is from my point of view, I'm going to advise you what's worked for me. Let your bad employees die!

Another part of the process is to hold regular sales meetings. This is an important part of the culture at our organization, even though it's commission-only. We want to build an inclusive environment, so we have a weekly sales meeting in which everyone gets the chance to speak.

The structure of the meeting begins with an informal conversation for a few minutes, to ensure that everyone is in the right frame of mind. Each salesperson provides specific updates on lead and lag measures (which we have discussed previously in the "Benchmark Stats" section of Chapter 3). Lead measures will be related to how many emails they have sent in a particular week, how many sales calls they have made, and how many proposals they've sent out. And then lag measures will be how sales are going, how many deals have been closed this week, and how the sales pipeline is looking.

If you get all of your people to speak in this way, you gain an overall impression of your entire organization. It also encourages your sales team to deliver, as no one wants to be the person in a meeting that admits they can't keep up. This meeting is sales-focused, and personnel issues should be dealt with on a one-on-one basis in different meetings. We hold our sales meeting weekly, and I don't recommend doing them first thing on Monday. Somewhere in the middle of the week, possibly Wednesday afternoon or Thursday morning, is ideal, some relatively dead time that isn't considered vital for the functioning of the organization. By scheduling the meeting this way, you free your salespeople to work first thing in the week, and crunch on Friday without distraction.

THE FOUR AGREEMENTS

One of my favorite books is "The Four Agreements" by Don Miguel Ruiz. One of the four agreements that he includes in this book is to be true to your word. And that means what it says. If you say that you are going to do something, do it. If you promise something, make sure that you live up to that promise. It's a simple credo by which I live my life. And it's the quickest and most powerful way to separate yourself from virtually every other person that you will encounter.

Because the vast majority of people say things, and then don't do them. Following through and living up to your commitments is important. In any field, you will find that the vast majority of people simply fail to do this. There are so many examples of this in everyday life. Try hiring someone to come to your house and clean for you, and you'll find out that even getting them to show up on time is difficult enough. That's before you go into actually doing the job!

That's why following through on your policies and commitments is critical. It's such a simple thing, yet it will separate you from the field as quickly as a Formula 1 car racing a pick-up truck. That means that if you say that you're going to write 40 cold emails this week, you make utterly sure that you actually do it. I don't care if you're writing them at 3 o'clock in the morning on a Saturday night, those emails are getting written and sent this week. And you keep delivering on that over and over and over again. Day after day after day, year after year after year, until it becomes second nature.

That's how you become a winner.

If you keep consistently hitting your numbers, keep following through on your promises, you'll win. It is 100% certain that the system outlined in this book will work, if you follow it with determination and diligence. That doesn't mean that it's easy. It's hard work. You will encounter obstacles. It can be disappointing at times. But if you commit to it, stick to it, and deliver what you have promised that you will, I can promise you that you will achieve massive success.

And this doesn't just apply to external promises, it's also the promises you tell yourself. I remember back when I was in college, I was trying to start a business and just couldn't get myself to work. I had problems motivating myself. I kept having great ideas, would think about them for a few days, then eventually think the once epic idea sucked, and I'd throw it away. Then, one day, I woke up at 2 o'clock in the morning, and I wrote down two words on a piece of paper:

Trust yourself.

I want everyone listening to this to do that as well. Because we all get hyped, we get excited about these great ideas that we have, yet something within us prevents us from following through on them. We don't follow our dreams. We allow ourselves to be tricked into a trapped existence, where we fall back into what's expected of us. The path of least resistance. If you can trust yourself, commit to following through on your ideas, you can change your life.

Another aspect of this is taking control of your own existence. I once encountered a successful salesperson who told me that whenever you're dealing with someone in the business realm, if something goes wrong you should always blame yourself. Even if the other party acted in a way that appears to be completely unreasonable, never complain, never shift the emphasis on to them, always blame yourself, and reflect on what you could've done differently. Even if you simply conclude that you need to choose better clients or partners.

If you make that distinction, then you're the person in control. It doesn't matter if someone else screws up, it doesn't matter if your client did everything wrong, you are the one that allowed this to happen. And you can then ensure that it doesn't happen again.

You will only reach your true potential in life if you trust yourself completely and make yourself fully responsible for your own outcomes.

CHAPTER 9.

Leading Your Team to Victory

A s we discussed in the previous chapter, cultivating your talent is important. And there are some broader leadership and management principles that are particularly important. You can give people the tools to succeed, but you won't truly enable them to reach their potential unless you manage them effectively.

In this chapter, we're going to talk about mindset traits and some practical things that you can implement as a leader that will improve your team, your business, your career, and ultimately your life. You shouldn't view what you do as a money-making exercise, you should aim to make a positive impact. So let's talk about that.

FOUR CRITICAL OBLIGATIONS

If you manage any sort of organization, you're always learning on the job and uncovering new things, but there are still broad principles you can put in place that will always apply and always deliver results. And your status as the manager is irrelevant to this. It doesn't matter if you're a junior manager, or the CEO of a massive company; these principles are universally applicable.

OBLIGATION TO THE EMPLOYEE

The first Obligation that you have is to the people that work with you. You want to make sure that they're happy, fulfilled, and that they feel they're on a positive career path. You might imagine that this requires something particularly proactive or disruptive. But I would argue the complete opposite. The way to fulfill this Obligation is to create a clean slate culture, in which you don't have any assumptions regarding anyone, and instead enable them to find their own way.

For example, I was talking to one of our team members, Jacob, recently. He is a sales guy within our organization, but he's also a talented YouTube content creator. And on his channel, he was making videos that were related to our sales process. Now, many companies would instantly be suspicious and even hostile towards such conduct. Big companies in particular tend to have a restrictive attitude to creating content. It would have been very easy for us to ask him to end it, and maybe even fire him. But instead of overreacting, what we did was engage with Jacob, and we found out that the reason he was making these videos is because he loves our sales training content.

Rather than telling him to stop, rather than inhibiting him as an individual, we enabled him. That's key to everything that you do as a sales leader and manager. Don't restrict. Enable.

So we actually gave him an editor, and offered him a percentage of sponsorship revenue from our main channel, trying to help him out with one of his passions. Just by offering him a little support, he is now more driven to perform within our organization. And that's a classic example of how you can motivate people, support people, and make sure that everyone is pulling the same way. It seems simple, but you'd be surprised how often even the most successful companies miss out on massive opportunities by doing the complete opposite. Apple, Google and Meta (Facebook) can afford to fire potential billionaires. You can't!

If you allow your employees to express themselves and be the people that they want to be, you will get far more out of them. Your employees will become more motivated and productive than you can possibly imagine. And they'll be happier. And wouldn't you rather oversee an organization with happy people rather than unhappy people?

OBLIGATION TO THE CUSTOMER

Of equal importance to your people are the customers. You must ensure that your customers believe in what you're doing. It must be clear what you're selling is not a scam, and that you deliver on your customer service promises — everything from providing functionality to refunds.

This applies at all levels of your organization.

For example, I sometimes make calls to my sales team to see how quickly the phone is answered. That's not checking up on them, it's ensuring that everything is functioning correctly. And I'm also gaining crucial insight into the customer's point of view. Effectively, your business only exists in the mind of the customer, so if they're having a bad experience then you're a bad company. So it's important to familiarize yourself with their perspective, even if you believe that you're doing an amazing job. It doesn't matter if you think you're doing a great job, if people who want to buy from you disagree!

OBLIGATION TO YOURSELF

Another important Obligation you have is to yourself. You want to make sure that you're excited to run your business. If you are doing things that excite you, you're inevitably going to perform better. But it's also your Obligation to create an environment in which people want to do the tasks that are assigned to them, in which you ensure that they have value and aren't morally dubious.

There are tasks that you need to perform sometimes that are neither inspiring nor interesting. But it only needs a small change in emphasis to get you motivated. For example, I film YouTube content regularly, I have a successful channel, yet I'm not always in the mood to shoot videos. Sometimes it just feels like I don't really care about the process.

But there are ways around this feeling. For example, recently I needed to shoot a batch of content, which were tutorial videos that were essentially rehashes of our sales training. And I really didn't want to do it! At all! I felt that it was already in the can, and that we were just going over old ground. It just wasn't that inspiring.

I needed to find a fix. And the solution was straightforward. I'll shoot the outros, have the team shorten the existing course videos, and then they effectively become a trailer for the sales training itself. As soon as I came up with this idea, I was able to film seven videos in about 30 minutes, because the psychological barrier was removed.

The important takeaway from this is that you can get super-excited about your job, and even some of the more tedious tasks that you have, just by tweaking the emphasis. And it's your job, your Obligation as a manager to ensure that you're excited about everything that you're doing. Because if you don't believe in what you're doing, if you're not motivated to deliver, then how can you expect people working with you to feel that drive?

OBLIGATION TO THE BUSINESS

The final critical Obligation of the manager is to the business itself. If your business isn't succeeding, then you won't succeed.

This works on multiple levels, but what I would particularly like to emphasize is that you need to create a positive culture. If you're part of a corporation, regardless of whether you're working for it or running it, and you're doing morally questionable things, in the long run you will struggle to succeed. Even if you do succeed, you won't feel like a success. So I always recommend to everyone, at every level of the company, to act as if they own the business. Act as if they have a stake in the reputation of the company.

When I first worked for the agency in New York, I was a junior sales guy. Another junior sales guy at the time was Michael Simpson (I changed his name to protect the innocent). What's the difference between myself and Michael Simpson today? I became the director of marketing and I'm now running my own corporation. The New York agency is still a client of ours and happy with what we're doing with them. And, half a decade later, Michael Simpson is still a junior salesperson.

That all happened because I decided to become the owner and to take ownership of the situation. It became increasingly obvious to me that I would rather run my own business than work for someone else. And so once I made that decision, I committed myself to investing all of my energy in doing things that would make the organization effective. And within a few months, the company was doing better than ever.

You have more power than anyone as a manager. You have the ability to build an effective business. The buck stops with you. If the business fails or underperforms, it's your fault. So always do everything possible to ensure that your business is effective and productive and that the working culture is exciting and rewarding. If you're working for a company and you get fired for doing this, it's absolutely fine. You should view this as an opportunity, a reward for prioritizing excellence. Now you can work for an organization that will truly value you and truly value what you do.

If your boss fires you for trying to make the organization better, you both deserve what happens next.

KEEPING THE BEST PEOPLE

I touched on this in the last section, but retaining the best people within your organization is critically important. An incredible number of businesses completely fail to keep their talent happy, and they let their star employees get away.

I've experienced this personally. When I was working with the New York agency, there was one particular day that remains etched on my mind. It was the day that I decided to become an entrepreneur. This wasn't due to some great plan that I had at the time, or any inherent ability that I possess. It was purely because of the way that I was treated.

On this particular day, I was speaking with the Director of Sales at the agency. And he asked me to write a list of my goals for the following year. So one of the goals that I came up with was to manage a team of interns within the next 12 months. When I presented him with this goal, he made a rather flippant joke. He said I wasn't ready. That perhaps in five years I might be able to manage a single intern.

And I decided right then that I was done. I was out of there. I'm not going to work somewhere that doesn't value me, or doesn't appreciate what I've done for the organization. So they lost their star employee. I fully believe that we could have generated hundreds of millions of dollars together. Everything that I've built with Robert, they could have had within their organization. I was fully committed to them, until I discovered that they weren't fully committed to me.

Simply by failing to allow the star employee to be a star, they lost this person completely. So this is something that we work on with our people all of the time. If you attract someone with talent, don't hold them back, enable them. Proactively work with them to ensure that they can reach their full potential.

One of my employees, Div Sharma, began working on my team as a virtual assistant in India. He wanted to do less assisting and make more video content, so I started letting him in on content creation. He began as an assistant, then started producing content on the Alex Berman channel, and now he is actually the manager of the Alex Berman brand, and he makes more money than the average doctor in India. Even more, he's on track to make six-figures annually, which is an unheard of salary in India, and I want him to reach that milestone as quickly as possible.

This all comes from retaining your star employees, supporting them in achieving their goals, and truly investing in their career path and outcomes. When I was talking to Jacob, who I mentioned in the previous section, one of the things I thought he could do is become the CEO of one of our SaaS companies. And I told him that I believed he could take it from zero to $30 million in revenue.

On the flip side, I remember that there was a news story about someone who was fired from Burger King for making TikTok and YouTube videos about the process of serving customers at the fast food chain. These videos were getting millions of views. So what happened? Well, he was fired. And within hours, he was hired by another fast food restaurant that now gets millions of views for their brand.

The bottom line is… if your star employee wants to manage a team of interns, or run their own YouTube channel, or make some videos on TikTok, or take on more responsibility, or leverage their skills in some way, let them do it. Encourage them to do it. Help your employees fulfill their dreams and ambitions and you'll achieve an unbelievable amount of buy-in and loyalty. You'll never lose them.

ALIGNING WITH COLD EMAIL

So how do you go about selling the cold email process internally?

There are three great ways that you can improve your sales organization. The first one is mission alignment — ensuring that everyone on your sales team knows why they're doing their jobs. If you have people that are only there for the money, they really shouldn't be in the organization, as everyone should understand the bigger picture behind what you're doing. This will make a huge difference.

For example, you might have a sales rep that has the opportunity to sell to an organization for $250,000. And all they're thinking about is how they will make a $25,000 commission as part of that process. Then you have a second salesperson who is selling the same product for $250,000, but not only will they earn the money, they've internalized how this product will change the organization and the lives of its customers. The second salesperson is far more likely to close the deal. Because they understand that what they're selling has value beyond monetary worth.

The second thing that works with cold email in particular is to get some competition going between salespeople. Let's say Jack booked 8 meetings. Great! But what if Jennifer booked 25? Suddenly, he has context for his performance and that context says he is an underperformer. By allowing your sales team to observe the sales performance of different people in the organization, you give them the opportunity to measure their own processes, ask questions and share best practices.

STARTING FROM SCRATCH

At this point, I'd like to talk about one of the most boring books ever written, so that you don't have to read it! The book in question is on management, and it's called "The Four Disciplines of Execution". It's an excellent book, it is full of superb ideas, but it is tremendously dull to read! So let's shrink it down for you.

One of the important concepts discussed in this book is lead measures and lag measures. We discussed these previously in the book, but it's important to implement them effectively in order to create a team that runs itself. And, of course, everyone wants to develop a team that runs itself, as they enable your operation to run like clockwork, and for you to focus your attention on more productive and creative activities.

The first step for creating a team that runs itself is to hire people that are already self-starters by nature. We'll talk about how you identify the right people shortly, but first let's discuss the second part of the process. That is to communicate to your people what they need to do, set your lead measures. Make clear what is a good number of cold emails to send weekly. And what is an acceptable number of sales calls to make. The minimum number of proposals that should be sent per week. Make sure that all of their targets are communicated to them clearly, so that they're just as aware of the benchmarks of the organization as you are.

And, actually, you'll find that it's easier to hire self-managed people if you get your team aligned with the mission, ensure that they are paid well, and that all the incentives are aligned for success. If you follow the principles outlined here, you'll make it easy for people to make money if they put in the work, and this inevitably attracts the best salespeople to your organization.

Absolutely key to this is ensuring that people don't feel like they have a boss. Who wants someone breathing over their shoulder all day? You want to feel like you're an autonomous individual, doing stuff that you really believe in, and that you're leveraging your skillset. That's way better than feeling like you're just following orders. Human beings have a natural inclination to seek freedom and liberation, so don't take this away from them by dispensing orders, create an organization in which people can manage themselves.

No one is telling me to write this book right now. No one is ordering Jacob to be the top sales person in the organization. No one is instructing Div to manage our YouTube channel. We're just doing it, we're just going for it, because we believe in and enjoy what we're doing.

Finally, there is an excellent way that you can identify people who will be aligned with this working culture. The one quality that I really value in people, and I try to embody myself, is delivering self-assigned work. If a candidate wants to write blog posts all day, but hasn't written their own blog, they aren't a good candidate. If you want to make YouTube content, but you haven't started your own YouTube channel, it's worth asking why.

That's what I look for during the hiring process. People that value themselves enough to not sit around. If I see somebody that's on Netflix every night, I don't want them in my organization. And that's not what the self-directed candidate is going to do. They're going to have worked a job for eight years, plus written three books, produced 100 YouTube videos, and have 200,000 followers on TikTok. They're going to be driven, they're going to have extracurricular activities and interests that are equally important, or even that outweigh, their day jobs.

Don't hire consumers. Hire creators. And be a creator.

COMPETITION INCREASES THE PERFORMANCE OF THE ORGANIZATION.

One of the hardest things to do is to get people to work faster. Some people are naturally quick, and will deliver rapidly, while others are inclined to be sluggish, and when you ask them to do something, they might say they'll deliver it, you follow up 1,000 times, and they eventually deliver it in six months. Adding this layer of competition to your processes helps leverage the maximum performance from your people, and makes it clear who needs to go.

The third important factor that I particularly value is bonuses. One of my mentors, Tom Tancredi, actually told me that people value a cash bonus more than a salary increase. They'd rather have a $2,000 cash bonus than a $500 monthly pay increase. This sounds insane, but it actually plays into a basic aspect of human psychology; people get used to salary increases over time. They never get used to random cash bonuses. This means cash bonuses cost you less and make your team happier.

So if you're able to offer people that instant incentive every so often, it can really be effective. But you have to give them a figure that makes them feel valued. One company that I worked for tried to incentivize us with $50 Amazon gift cards. Not only is that an insulting amount of money, it's not even a cash payment. I don't think I even claimed my gift card in the end! You can't have people closing six-figure deals, and then not even give them enough money to buy one video game from Amazon!

Of course, any bonus has to be in the context of your organization and salary payments, I aim for $1,000 as I want people to sit up and pay attention. And, fundamentally, you're doing this to make people feel valued, so that they'll go the extra mile. What could be worse than giving people a bonus that makes them feel insulted? You just had to pay money, and now they're mad at you. No. Give a bit more to actually get the result you want.

In line with this, it's destructive to impose stringent requirements on your people. Your ethos should always be — let them do whatever they want (within reason!). For instance, when I was the salesperson in New York, although there was a dress code for most employees, the people in our department were allowed to wear whatever we wanted. And the clothes that people chose to wear varied quite considerably. Someone that sat next to me wore a suit every day. Another guy would wear a collared shirt. I looked up to the people in Silicon Valley, so I performed better in the typical San Francisco billionaire attire of a plain black t-shirt.

Simply by the company allowing us to be comfortable, we felt better and performed better. It created an enabling and supportive vibe for the company, rather than creating a needlessly dictatorial atmosphere.

PROACTIVE COMPENSATION

The final thing that I want to discuss in this chapter is engaging your whole team in deciding their compensation.

Most people know what they want. They just need the permission to ask for it. But what most bosses do is the following:

Hey, guys, we have this new initiative, we're going to be sending 1,000 cold emails each week. Let me know when that's done. I want 1,000 emails out by the end of the week ASAP.

That's one way to approach it. Here's another approach:

Hey, guys, we've got this new initiative to send cold emails, because it's going to really improve the organization, and we're going to book a bunch of meetings. How many emails do you think is realistic to send in one week?

By asking the employees what they think is realistic, you might get an array of different answers. They might say 20! But then you can have a discussion with them, and engage them in the decision-making process. "Most teams deliver 1,000. You think you can only do 20?". Immediately, they have more ownership.

This relates to compensation as well. Instead of telling people what they're going to be paid, you can instead ask them what they consider to be fair compensation based on the budget. Again, this feeds into the whole concept of making people feel valued, of enabling them, and always engaging them with the business. You're not just treating them as workhorses, who will grind themselves into the dust for the business, you're truly involving them in the process. They are stakeholders.

And it's possible that your salespeople will even ask for a lower commission than you were willing to pay. It can be a win-win situation. The important thing is that by simply involving your employees in the discussion, you ensure that they feel valued, which is precisely the opposite approach to the discussion that I had in New York that led to me becoming an entrepreneur. You don't want that. You don't want your best people walking out to do their own thing. You want them working with you forever.

So if you've learned anything from this chapter, it's that people will do whatever they're going to do, regardless of whether you're there or not. Therefore, your job as manager is to identify the people that will flourish within your organization, and create an enabling culture that allows them to succeed. It's not your job as manager to change people, make people do things that they don't want to do, or, crucially, that they don't believe in. You're in the talent identification business and the hype business!

And if you can identify the right people, and get them excited about working with you, the sky's the limit!

CHAPTER 10.

Other Uses for Cold Email

If you've listened to the book to this point, you know how to use cold email to transform your sales and your business. We're pretty much done with the meat and potatoes of that process now. So in this chapter, I want to talk about how you can use cold email to achieve all sorts of different things — from generating backlinks for SEO, to getting a dream job, and more. As part of this process, I'll share some scripts, along with some other ways that we've used cold email to win. Hopefully, this will inspire you to embark on your own cold email journey. I want to prove to you that cold email is a superpower that will change everything about your life.

GENERATING BACKLINKS

First, let's talk about an email template for generating backlinks. Cold email is a great tool for getting other companies and valuable sources to link to your website. It's a fantastic way to get people to talk about you, and it's an excellent vehicle for promotion. In case you don't know about backlinks, from an SEO point of view these are really valuable, as backlinks mean that someone else has directly linked to your website via their site. This will typically help you rank higher on Google, generating more traffic as a result. And it will also help you get featured on their website, generating more traffic as a result. We've used this strategy to get featured in Forbes, Entrepreneur, The Huffington Post, and hundreds of other publications.

Before we go over the cold email that you can use to get backlinks, I want to talk a little about mindset. Why would anyone choose to give you a backlink? Well, it's primarily because they need content on their website. So if you go in and pitch valuable work, aligned with their existing content, then you're actually saving them time. Journalists are usually hungry for content, so if you present yourself the right way, you're offering them something of value, and you end up becoming the topic of their work.

I would also recommend only following up twice to reduce spam complaints. Just the main email, then a bump, and then a final query. So let's talk about the email template that worked for us when we were looking for backlinks.

> Subject: Quick Question
> Hey Mark, big fan of everything you, loved the article about xyz.
> Noticed you've written about Dotomator before, so I figured you'd find this useful. I built an alternative to dotomator called browsedomains.com
>
> I used to use Dotomator, but found that it needed more keywords and categories to be useful.
>
> If you find the tool helpful, it would mean the world to me if you can share it on your website!
>
> Thanks,
> Alex

To give you some more insight on this process, at one time we were seeking backlinks for a tool we built called BrowseDomains. This was an improvement over an existing tool. This meant that when we were seeking backlinks, we simply contacted everyone that had previously linked to the older tool, and many of them were receptive to our approach. You could easily implement this strategy with your own business. There is probably a famous brand or person in your industry that is outdated, or a successful software product that could be improved upon. Tell people that have back linked them that you're doing the same thing, but doing it better.

This is highly effective. It's basically free PR.

ALL ABOUT PODCASTS

Another great way to use cold email to build your brand quickly is to target podcasts, and to host your own podcast. If you can set this up, you can talk to leaders in your space, heroes in your industry, and gain massive traction in the process. In this section, I want to talk about how we've done that, and how you can achieve a similar outcome.

But, first, why is podcasting great for your brand? Two reasons. First, if you appear on other people's podcasts, their audience already has a relationship with them. So this enables you to get in front of an established audience, an audience that you can understand and identify before the podcast, and build a relationship with them. And this is achieved in a way that doesn't really happen with blog posts or tweets, because you're there for a long period of time, hyping your product, in a concerted way.

This means that it's very useful to get on other people's podcasts. I've been on hundreds — everything from Leadpages to Entrepreneur on Fire. In fact, if you name a business podcast, you can guarantee I've either been on it, or tried to get on it! And it's been amazing for us. Imagine being able to say that you were on your hero's podcast, imagine meeting the people that you admire, and speaking with them for an hour. Even if you only make a minimal amount of sales as a result, being on a top podcast is valuable for the simple reason that you're learning from your heroes.

The first part of this process is writing an email draft for podcasts. This requires research — make sure that all of the podcasts you're targeting have talked about similar things to your topic previously. It's important to note that podcasting is a very mature space compared to even five years ago. There are niche podcasts for anything and everything. So you can really identify something that suits your needs. If you're a web design agency, talk to agency growth podcasts, or web design podcasts, or even coding podcasts.

Step two is to identify relevant podcast episodes to call out. As with all cold emails, you want to make sure that you're customizing, and one of the easiest ways to customize is to acknowledge some content that they've recorded in the past.

Here's the script:

Subject: Quick question
Hey Jack, loved the interview that you did with Dan Smith.

I'm head of growth for a company called x27. We do fully managed sales and lead generation for B2B companies. Naturally, we're trying to get the word out :)

Since we target a similar group, I think it'd be interesting for your audience to hear some of these insights:

- How we hire and vet candidates
- How we use cold emails for our recruiter clients to find interested companies, including email scripts and the exact targeting

Does that sound interesting? Happy to workshop some ideas as well.

Thanks,
Alex

Notice what we're doing in this email. We're coming to them. We're saying that we're fans of their show. And we're giving them specific things that they could talk about. This email was hugely successful; it had a 30% positive response rate. That's the power of a cold email script. If you were to hire a podcasting agency, they might book you 30 podcasts over a year, whereas you could do this for yourself via 100 emails, without spending a cent.

The second part of this process is getting somebody on your podcast. One of the best things that I've been able to achieve with cold email is meet almost anybody I want — everyone from major authors, to gigantic Hollywood producers, to business leaders, and authors whose work I admire. Cold email has brought me into contact with an extremely diverse range of prestigious people. These people will make time for me because I have a podcast. By starting a podcast, you're able to connect with anyone you want, even if they don't have a show. And it's not that hard to get them.

You can use cold email to meet with anyone. The other day, I was watching a video with my brother Jacob about Barack Obama's former chef. And we emailed the chef and he got back to us to coordinate a charity event! We didn't end up going through with the charity event but he did respond.

So how do you go about this process? Step one is the usual research! Make sure that you know the background of the person in question, and provide ideas for discussion; the same way that you would customize your outreach. Here is an example of a script that you could use:

Subject: Quick question
Hey Owen,
Big fan of the content. You basically changed my little brother's life. Huge fan. He's been sending me videos of yours for years.

I run a podcast and often talk to successful entrepreneurs, and people doing cool stuff. Would love to learn from you. Want to do an interview?

Let me know and I can send over a few times.

Cheers,
Alex

You can go out and make a list of your heroes right now, and start signing them up for your podcast with cold email. And the best thing is that the script can be used via social media platforms, so you can DM them on Twitter, Instagram, or anywhere else. Find the platform that the influencers are on, and send them a message outlining your proposal.

GETTING YOUR DREAM JOB

I know this works because I got my first job via cold email! I was in Naples, Florida. I knew absolutely nobody, but I wanted a job in New York or San Francisco. And I got that job by sending cold emails. So let me show you the exact template that I used to book that initial coffee meeting with Joe Ziemer from Betterment.

> Subject: CM Question
>
> Hi Joe,
>
> I was doing some research on content manager positions at NY startups. And I noticed you're a manager at Betterment. I also checked you on Twitter and notice we both like the song: "You can call me Al".
>
> I'm on a quest for my dream job and would love to ask you three to five questions about your experience working for Betterment. Would you be available for a quick chat over coffee this Thursday at 10am?
>
> I'm also free anytime Friday.

Sincerely,

Alex Berman

PS. I'm sure you're busy. So if it's easier for you, I'd be happy to send my questions via email. Thanks again.

That was a very early effort for me, so there are a few things that I would tweak. I wouldn't say "CM" in the subject line, because the recipient wouldn't know what that means without opening the email. Nonetheless, as we've refined the approach, we've used this strategy consistently and not just for my own jobs. I helped my brother Joseph get a job at one of the top record labels in LA. I also helped my friend Fernando get a job at his dream architecture firm in Dallas. So this works in any niche.

Go out there and get your dream job. Get any job you want. Cold email is a great way to get hired because it's proactive, meaning you're not stuck waiting to hear back from your hiring manager, you're actually going out there and getting what you want. It's also personal and it's directed straight to the decision maker. I am a huge fan of personal responsibility. And I am hugely against anything that is cookie-cutter, or that involves following society's rules. So any time that you can break the rules, and just go directly to the person that you'll be working for, I'd say do it. It's going to get you hired.

And, third, cold email is going to make an impression, regardless of what happens if you don't get the job. For example, I didn't get the job at Betterment! But because

I sent that email to Joe, he became a connection, and he introduced me to a ton of people that worked at a bunch of other companies around New York City. He basically ushered me into the New York startup scene! I knew nobody; suddenly I knew somebody important, and he got me right in there. So even if you don't get the job, you can still win. That's the perfect form of business strategy.

So here's what you need to keep in mind. Say directly what you like about the company, and be very specific. When I wrote to Joe, I outlined definite roles that I was looking for; i.e. content manager. I didn't state that I was available for any roles at Betterment, because that puts too much onus on them to find your position, or place you in a certain context. So know exactly what you want, and call it out in the email itself.

You should also go straight for your future boss. A lot of people think you should go through HR. That's completely incorrect. If your boss has a candidate they want then that candidate will get hired. The company doesn't want to assign some random person to your boss; if the boss already has a good candidate, there's no world in which that makes sense! Talk to your boss like (s)he's a person and get hired by them directly, and you can actually get higher salaries and more prominent roles than HR would ever allow.

Also, just focus on getting to the meeting. You're not trying to get a job outright with this cold email, you just want to meet this person. You want a chance to have coffee and to feel them out. And at that meeting, you can ask them questions about the job. And if they like you then you get hired. It's as simple as that. For example, when Fernando applied for the architect job, it was under the guise of getting feedback on his portfolio, because he was graduating with an Architecture degree. The guy who met with him gave him feedback on his portfolio. And the obvious next step was...your portfolio is excellent, do you want a job? You're meeting with the top architect, and you have a great portfolio, why wouldn't he hire you?! Fernando still has that job to this day — one cold email has set up his entire career.

ACHIEVING ANYTHING

This chapter has outlined a few ways that you can use cold email. But I want you to think about other ways that you could implement it. It's not just a tool for sales. I want you to break out of that mindset.

You can literally do whatever you want. That's what I want to get across. Cold email does not *solely* mean emailing people to book sales meetings for your business. Cold email means crafting your pitch in a way to get what you want from whoever you want.

And that's what I really want to sink in. If one thing sinks in from this book, then this is the most important. There are no barriers between you and anybody that you want to meet. Just craft your pitch, send it to their direct email, and see what happens.

Thanks for reading.

CHAPTER 11.

Where To Go From Here

You understand that cold email is a life-changing and business-changing skill. You also know how to use cold email to open up new channels for your company, how to acquire unlimited sales, and how to hire your team. You can use cold email to get a dream job, to generate unlimited hype for your business, to achieve endless goals. We've even gone over some important tips on leadership, management, growing your company, and developing the best mindset to succeed.

At this point, all you have to do is execute. You have everything that you need in order to get whatever you want. So go do it.

Build your lead list, assemble your sales team, spin your marketing up using the criteria that we have outlined. You can even copy and paste the exact scripts that we've included in this book. You can follow the exact process to the letter, and you will generate huge amounts of money. If you're a freelancer in India making $400 per month, use this as a stepping stone to getting a job in America and making $4,000. Or if money isn't what you desire, you can create unlimited opportunities, start a charity, achieve whatever your most esteemed goal is with this system.

I hope you're as excited by the prospect as I am for you, because I know that so many people are going to achieve so much having listened to this book. I'm just grateful that I discovered how effective cold email can be, and how it can unlock everything that you wish to achieve in life. Whatever your situation is, cold email can deliver it for you. It doesn't matter if you're a one-man or one-woman creative business, or a vast corporation employing thousands. It doesn't matter if you're rich or poor, where you live in the world, what your life experience has been, or what you're trying to achieve... cold email can help you! That's why it's so valuable.

ADDITIONAL RESOURCES

So the next step is to get going with cold email. You have everything that you need now. But before you begin, I wanted to provide one final portion of additional resources.

First, there are several people you can follow via social platforms:

- Alex Berman would be a great place to start! I'm big on YouTube and Twitter.
- You can check out my channel at YouTube.com/AlexBerman, or Alex Berman on Twitter.
- You can also follow some of the greats, such as Steli Efti, Aaron Ross, Will Cannon, and Sujan Patel. That's quite enough for anyone.

Second, courses and consulting can be extremely helpful. With this in mind, we have published a suite of courses on our website. These are available via ColdEmail-Manifesto.com/courses.

If you want to work with others in a consulting capacity, you should go to AlexBerman.com/agency. I look forward to taking your business to the next level; our team is ready to help you in any way possible. If you want to do things for yourself, please sign up for the course. Or if you want us to grow your company for you, as we've achieved with hundreds of clients in the past, our agency is the place to go.

NO EXCUSES

You now have everything that you could ever conceivably need. You have no excuses. You can begin to implement cold email today, and unlock untold success and riches. The only barrier to achieving this is yourself. You have to be invested in the process.

We have now tested this process with over 80,000 people via our YouTube channel, Twitter, and via our training suite. We know for a fact that this is the easiest, fastest, and best way to generate more clients for your business.

You don't need any other book. You don't need any other information. There aren't any other podcasts, channels or courses that will provide anything additional to what we've given you. All of the data and expertise is at your fingertips. We put everything in here that could possibly be required. And, to reiterate, we've given it away at a pretty affordable price!

So you have no more excuses. We've made it possible for you to succeed. And I genuinely don't want you to look back on this several years from now, and realize that you had the answer to all of your problems and conundrums, but never acted on this information. You're ready to achieve massive success at this very moment, if you want it.

Don't be too stubborn. Don't be too lazy. Understand the power and potential of what you have in your hands right now. Cold email is the key to solving every revenue issue that you have ever experienced in your business. All you have to do is send some emails.

You have nothing to lose and everything to gain. Go do it. Right now.

LINKS:

All of our cold email tools:
ColdEmailManifesto.com/tools

Courses to grow your business:
ColdEmailManifesto.com/courses

Free proposal template:
ColdEmailManifesto.com/proposal

All of our cold email scripts:
ColdEmailManifesto.com/inbox

Free Sales Training:
Youtube.com/AlexBerman

Done for You:
AlexBerman.com/Agency

ABOUT THE AUTHORS:

Alex Berman: Youtube creator. Founder of Leadshark, Taplio, X27. Managing Partner at A&R. Known for sales training and teaching as the Cold Email King. Over 100k followers across social media channels.

Robert Indries: CEO of 8 profitable businesses generating 7-figures yearly, including cold email and lead generation firm x27.

Alex and Robert's teams have collectively produced hundreds of millions of dollars using cold email and want to help you to do the same.

A free ebook edition is available with the purchase of this book.

To claim your free ebook edition:

1. Visit MorganJamesBOGO.com
2. Sign your name CLEARLY in the space
3. Complete the form and submit a photo of the entire copyright page
4. You or your friend can download the ebook to your preferred device

Print & Digital Together Forever.

Snap a photo

Free ebook

Read anywhere

Printed in the USA
CPSIA information can be obtained
at www.ICGtesting.com
JSHW022338140824
68134JS00019B/1562